Folk Dancing

Erica M. Nielsen

The American Dance Floor
Ralph G. Giordano, Series Editor

GREENWOOD

AN IMPRINT OF ABC-CLIO, LLC
Santa Barbara, California • Denver, Colorado • Oxford, England

Library of Congress Cataloging-in-Publication Data

Nielsen, Erica M.
   Folk dancing / Erica M. Nielsen.
       p. cm. — (The American dance floor)
   Includes bibliographical references and index.
   ISBN 978-0-313-37688-7 (hardcopy : alk. paper) — ISBN 978-0-313-37689-4
(ebook)   1. Folk dancing.   2. Country-dances.   I. Title.
   GV1743.N47   2011
   793.3—dc22   2011014690

ISBN: 978-0-313-37688-7
EISBN: 978-0-313-37689-4

15 14 13 12 11   1 2 3 4 5

This book is also available on the World Wide Web as an eBook.
Visit www.abc-clio.com for details.

Greenwood
An Imprint of ABC-CLIO, LLC

ABC-CLIO, LLC
130 Cremona Drive, P.O. Box 1911
Santa Barbara, California 93116-1911

This book is printed on acid-free paper ∞

Manufactured in the United States of America

Folk Dancing

*For my husband, Nicholas Okamura, who makes my
heart dance with joy.*

Contents

Series Foreword

From the Lindy Hop to hip hop, dance has helped define American life and culture. In good times and bad, people have turned to dance to escape their troubles, get out, and have a good time. From high school proms to weddings and other occasions, dance creates some of our most memorable personal moments. It is also big business, with schools, competitions, and dance halls bringing in people and their dollars each year. And as America has changed, so, too, has dance. The story of dance is very much the story of America. Dance routines are featured in movies, television, and videos; dance styles and techniques reflect shifting values and attitudes toward relationships; and dance performers and their costumes reveal changing thoughts about race, class, gender, and other topics. Written for students and general readers, The American Dance Floor series covers the history of social dancing in America.

Each volume in the series looks at a particular type of dance such as swing, disco, Latin, folk dancing, hip hop, ballroom, and country & western. Written in an engaging manner, each book tells the story of a particular dance form and places it in its historical, social, and cultural context. Thus each title helps the reader learn not only about a particular dance form, but also about social change. The volumes are fully documented, and each contains a bibliography of print and electronic resources for further reading.

Preface

The United States is home to a large array of dance forms representative of the many types of people who have populated the land. Some dance forms are affiliated with different nationalities or ethnicities and were either created abroad or by immigrants living in the United States. Other dance forms such as Square Dance, in all its variations, are considered American because they developed on American soil and have unique characteristics that distinguish them from other nations' dance forms. Dance forms such as the Waltz and the Polka are so well known that Americans embrace them as their own dances even though these dances originated elsewhere. The term "folk dance" commonly describes any dance form tied to a specific cultural group or nationality.

In the early 20th century, social reformers and professional educators in England and the United States introduced European folk dances to children and immigrants in settlements, schools, playgrounds, and after-school programs. Around the time of World War I, the folk dance movement grew to include rural American dance forms. Then, in the 1930s and 1940s, a surge in fairs and festivals introduced countless people to folk dancing. Soon after, folk dance clubs, weekend dance events, and weeklong dance camps brought people together and facilitated the development of nationwide networks of enthusiasts. The folk dance movement flourished after World War II with increased record production and a folk music revival, and it peaked when the baby boomers reached adulthood in the 1960s and 1970s.

This book begins with a discussion about classifying dance forms and different interpretations of "folk dance." Chapters 1 and 2 provide an overview of Native American dances and African American dances to help contextualize the relationship of these forms to the folk dance movement. Chapter 3 summarizes European immigration to the New World and describes European dance forms that were popular through the end of the 19th century. European dance forms make up the bulk of early folk dance repertoire, and European ballroom dances heavily influenced American rural dance forms, or American folk dance.

Chapter 4 situates the folk dance movement within the context of Progressive era urban social reform initiatives. It delves into the history of gymnastics and gymnastics dancing in education, and it discusses folk dancing as a means to assimilate immigrants, improve children's well-being, and reinforce the Anglo national spirit. Chapter 5 explores American folk dance activities and shows how Square Dance spread from rural areas to cities as a type of recreation. Chapters 6 through 8 provide an overview of International Folk Dance, Modern Western Square Dance, and Contra Dance. An examination of these dance communities sheds light on related dance forms, including Balkan Dance, Clogging, English Country Dance, Israeli Dance, Line Dance, Round Dance, and Scottish Country Dance. Finally, the conclusion summarizes the folk dance movement and examines its contemporary state.

My first experience with International Folk Dance was in 2003 at age 22. I had never encountered Square Dance or Contra Dance prior to conducting fieldwork for this book in 2008–2010. During my journey, I interacted with hundreds of dancers and attended numerous regularly scheduled dances, dance weekends, and dance camps. As a dance anthropologist, I attempted to write objectively from the cultural insiders' point of view, while addressing questions that were intriguing to me as a cultural outsider, such as the following:

What makes a dance a "folk dance"?

Does the United States have original folk dances?

Where and how have people experienced folk dance?

Why is the label "folk dance" tied strongly to European dance forms?

What type of person is attracted to folk dance?

A timeline at the beginning of the book outlines important events that led up to and shaped the folk dance movement. A glossary provides definitions of dance forms and related concepts. A reference section shows readers where to seek further information. Finally, an index enables readers to quickly locate information on dance forms, events, key players, and major themes.

Research for this project was funded in part by the New Leaders, Good Leaders Fund of the Country Dance and Song Society, the Arizona Commission on the Arts, and the Stockton Folk Dance Camp. Hundreds of people contributed through formal interviews, informal conversations, emails, surveys, resource donations, carpools, and home-stays. Mentioning everyone would be an impossible task, but I deeply value all the contributors. Some interviewees are quoted, but even interviewees who are not quoted helped shape the scope of this book by drawing my attention to important themes. The people who participated demonstrated heartwarming generosity and passion. I am honored to be able to represent them to the best of my ability in this work.

Abundant thanks goes to Ron Houston of the Society of Folk Dance Historians for his overall mentorship throughout the writing process. Both he and Anthony Shay assisted with the organization of the International Folk Dance content. Furthermore, I am indebted to several other International Folk Dance (and Balkan dance, Scandinavian dance, etc.) enthusiasts for taking time to teach me about their activities, particularly Carolyn Allenby, Ed Austin, Sunni Bloland, JoAnne Clemens, LeJeune Decker, Susan Droz, Nelda Drury, Jerry Duke, Kristina Efimenko, Ann Eskayo, Oscar Faoro, Bill and Karen Faust (and their group in Tucson, Arizona), John Filcich, Connie Jahrmarkt, Eden Kaiser, Athan Karras, Craig Kurumada, Jaap Leegwater, Roo Lester, Michael Levinsky, Lynn Maners, Larry Miller, Bruce Mitchell, Yves Moreau, Sean and Una O'Farrell, Lee Otterholt, Lois Postel, and Nancy Lee Ruyter, and Richard E. Watt.

Clark Baker and Allan Hurst provided valuable editorial feedback based on their experience with Modern Western Square Dance. Bill Eyler contributed his insights to the Line Dance section, and Jeff Driggs, Sharon Lopeman, and Katie Popiel contributed to the Clogging section. During my research, other people who enhanced my understanding of Square Dance include, but are not limited to, David Anderson, Bob Brundage, Sandie Bryant, Stephen Cole, James Coull, Dane Cormac, Marshall Flippo, Rick Gittelman, Bill Harrison, Jerry Helt Kris Jensen, Gene Lauze, David Lefton, William "Doc" Litchman, Seth

Levine, Gordon Macaw, Tom Miller, William Napier, Tony Parkes, Bette and Ray Saltzmann, Betty and Ted Vaile, and Bernie and Evelyn Weber. Additionally, Phil Jamison and Alan Winston helped me grasp and articulate the complicated evolution of European and American Square Dance forms.

Bob Dalsemer, David Millstone, and Stephanie Smith helped with the Contra Dance chapter. In the field, I learned about the Contra Dance and related communities from several other individuals, including Sam Bartlett, David Cantieni, Brian Chase, Marian Clark, Shane Clark, Johnathan Domash, Rachel Fifer, Stan Fowler, Ethan Hazzard-Watkins, Stuart Hean, Joe and Peg Hesley, Steve Hickman, Abby Ladin, Kappy Laning, Bob McQuillen, Elvie Miller, Olivia Padovan, Nathan Paine, Ann Percival, David Roodman, Brad Saylor, Susan Schreiber, John Michael Seng-Wheeler, David Shewmaker, Charlotte Swavola, and John Wheeler. The writing process was very challenging, and I could not have completed this work without their help.

I would like to express gratitude toward my family and friends as well as the team at Tigerfish Transcription for their support and encouragement. Finally, I extend my appreciation to ABC-CLIO/Greenwood for taking a chance on a young researcher who had long dreamed of accomplishing such a project. I am indebted to editors George Butler and Ralph G. Giordano as well as the rest of the team at ABC-CLIO/ Greenwood who worked on the book for their motivation, expertise, and suggestions. Any errors, mischaracterizations, or omissions are my own and should not be attributed to anyone else who participated.

Timeline

1100 BC–146 BC	Ancient Greece; dancing is part of education and life
509 BC–AD 476	Ancient Rome; dancing is essential to festivities
1st–4th century	Christian worship incorporates dancing
5th–15th century	European Middle Ages; dancing for worship gradually is secularized
15th–16th century	European Renaissance; dancing is popularized by royal courts
17th century	North American colonists imitate English and French court dances
18th century	Contradanse Française and Cotillon, ancestors of American Square Dance, sweep across European and American ballrooms
19th century	The Quadrille and closed-position couple dances enter ballrooms
	A variety of Square Dance styles develop in rural American communities
1890s–1920s	Progressive era; folk dancing is taught mainly to children and immigrants
1920s–1930s	Folk dancing is recognized as wholesome recreation for everyone
1940s–1950s	Recreational folk dance clubs spread across North America

1960s–1970s   Rural community dances decline

Modern Western Square Dance begins

International Folk Dance focuses on Balkan dance

Contra Dance gains a large following

1980s–1990s   School folk dance programs and recreational folk dance clubs decline

1990s–2010s   Modern technologies facilitate communication among vast networks of folk dance enthusiasts

Introduction

In most parts of the world, dance is meaningfully incorporated into life events. Cultural beliefs and values influence how dance happens in terms of physical setting, who participates, musical accompaniment, attire, and accessories. For instance, many Christian societies celebrate the pre-Lent period of Carnival, but in different ways. In Brazil, neighborhood Samba schools or dance groups spend up to a year constructing costumes and floats to compete in a grand parade. Yaqui *pascola*, or dancers, from northern Mexico and the southwestern United States adorn themselves with deer hides and antlers for a ritual known as Danza del Venado. For Mardi Gras in New Orleans, a variety of dance forms, including Two-Step and Zydeco, happen alongside feasting and bead exchange in taverns and clubs and on the street. Dance is always tied to culture, and specifically how people choose to express themselves through dance comes from longstanding tradition as well as their life experiences in a given time and place.

Dance is labeled as "social dance" when the primary purpose is to interact with people in a fun recreational setting, with or without formal instruction. Throughout history, social dance has been a way to show off status, meet potential spouses or partners, or simply relax after a long day. Social dance may be preferred by people who yearn for a fun, visceral mind-body experience, or by people who feel awkward in other types of recreational activities that entail more verbal conversation. Many school, college, and community fitness programs have social dance classes for health and fitness as well. For over a century, philosophers and dance educators have stated that dance can improve personal demeanor and benefit society overall, because supposedly people who learn to move smoothly on the dance floor will be gracious in everyday life.

There is no definite explanation as to why humans gain pleasure from engaging in stylized movement to rhythm for celebration and self-expression. In *Dancing in the Streets: A History of Collective Joy* (2006), Barbara Ehrenreich suggests that dance is universally encoded in humans in a way similar to erotic love, music, color, and feasting (2006, 260). Dance is part of our collective heritage, a pleasurable practice that may be as old as the human race. Yet, throughout history, dance also has sparked much controversy. It has been banned during religious movements where activities and particularly pleasures of the flesh that distracted people from work and worship were considered immoral. In North America, widespread fear of dance cultivated by antidance exponents and the popularization of dance as a feminine activity have reduced the status of dance to something frivolous unless it involves professional training.

Several 20th-century anthropologists, including Franz Boas and Gertrude Kurath, have been intrigued by the function of dance in society. Their work illustrates at a scholarly level the natural human desire to attribute meaning to motion. To facilitate discussions about dance and culture, dance scholars have used labels such as ritual dance, theatrical dance, traditional dance, fad dance, popular dance, folk dance, national dance, character dance, and ethnic dance. Labeling dance forms is useful as long as it does not imply that some dance forms are superior to others. Problematically, assuming that certain dance forms are inferior may imply that the people who practice them are inferior as well.

A ritual dance has spiritual significance where the purpose is to communicate with a greater power to achieve a bountiful harvest, fertility, recovery from in injury or illness, or another desirable outcome. It gives people a way to deal with forces that seem beyond their comprehension and control, and the participants are not necessarily concerned about aesthetics. Conversely, a theatrical dance is intended to be aesthetic. It entails feats of precision, flexibility, strength, and speed acquired through years of rigorous training. In North America, thousands of dance studios offer this type of dance training in preparation for dance competitions and recitals.

When a dance form endures over time, it is known as traditional. A traditional dance is passed from generation to generation and may be so old that its origins are uncertain. At the other end of the spectrum are short-lived fads. One of the most famous North American fad dances was the Twist, popularized by Chubby Checker's cover of Hank Ballard's song in 1960. Popular dances are well known to the public and can be longstanding traditions or temporary fads.

A folk dance can be cross-labeled as a social dance if its main purpose is fun recreation, as a ritual dance if it has spiritual (usually pre-Christian) significance, or as a theatrical dance if it is choreographed for an audience and uses folksy peasant motifs. As either a social dance or a ritual dance, a folk dance can be a traditional dance or a fad dance. Popular dance forms of yesterday generally become the folk dances of today. Historically, folk dancing provides an alternative to contemporary dance forms that are popular in part because they push boundaries and offer something new and perhaps controversial.

A folk dance can be called a national dance if it is well known throughout a nation and is believed to symbolize a people's national spirit. Some examples include the Tarantella of Italy, the Hambo of Sweden, the Csárdás of Hungary, and the Kolo of Serbia. Many Americans consider Square Dance to be the national dance of the United States. "Square Dance" refers to a dance form with many regional styles for groups of male-female couples in circle, square, and line formations. It primarily evolved from the European court dances brought by early settlers and was tied to rural community life before recreational Square Dance clubs appeared in the 20th century.

National dances can fall into the genres of social, ritual, and even theatrical. Many nations have their own national folk music and dance ensembles, but these ensembles' performances or exhibitions rarely are exact replications of the dance practices of the nationals who are supposed to be represented. Choreographers usually adapt social dances or ritual dances to make them more aesthetic and glamorous.

Recreational folk dancers sometimes use the terms "village dance," "folkloric dance," or "ethnic dance" for a social or ritual type of folk dance, and "composed dance" or "character dance" for a theatrical type of folk dance. A character dance depicts a particular persona through movement, attire, props, and music. Professional folk dancers, who are usually trained in ballet, often portray the characters of happy and hard-working peasants when performing onstage. Early folk dance teachers in American schools were known to teach character dances, and some early folk dance manuals did not distinguish between folk dance and character dance.

Recreational folk dancers may participate in exhibition groups, but their overarching goal is noncompetitive social fun. Their main venue is the regularly scheduled dance, which sometimes is named for when it occurs, such as the Monday Dance or the Second Wednesday Dance (of the month). Many dancers supplement their regularly scheduled dance experience with special events such as folk dance festivals, dance weekends, and dance camps. The majority of folk dancers participate in more than one dance form, and there is some disagreement over which dance forms actually are folk dances.

"Folk dance" often is a label given to dances that are brought out of their original social context and used for education, recreation, or exhibition. For instance, a Bulgarian who dances in a churchyard for a saint's day celebration considers the activity to be social dancing or simply dancing, not folk dancing. Yet a folk dance teacher from North America may teach the same dance to a group of folk dancers, and it becomes recognized as a folk dance in the new context. Perceptions about what defines a folk dance changed substantially over the 20th century, and currently, quite often, folk dance is defined loosely as any dance "of the people."

Dance forms are not static; they move across time and space, they adopt new classifications and meanings, and they naturally change. The process of change is not always clear. Some dance forms are reshaped to such a degree and are undocumented for such a long time that tracing their roots presents an enormous challenge.

1

Native American Dances

Prior to the arrival of Europeans in the New World, the indigenous tribes of the Americas had a range of dance forms as diverse as their languages, traditions, beliefs, and lifestyles. Their ritual dances occurred for specific reasons in spiritually meaningful settings, and these rituals used natural resources for instruments, props, and attire. Some dances required specific chants and ingestible substances or a lack thereof. Many indigenous dance forms were lost after the arrival of Europeans, sometimes because entire tribes were eradicated by foreign diseases and warfare, and also because Europeans perceived the Native Americans as savages and went to great lengths to suppress their cultures (Chujoy 1949, 10–14; Needham 2002, 16–20).

In the 19th century, American pioneers of European heritage claimed the majority of land west of the Mississippi River, land that the U.S. government had promised to Native Americans. The pioneers went west for different reasons: to escape overcrowded cities on the East Coast, to join the California gold rush, to claim land, to seek adventure, to flee religious persecution, or to make a living in industries such as ranching, mining, and railroading. During westward expansion, pioneers had conflicts with Native Americans. In the 1870s, the U.S. government supported the mass slaughter of buffalo in attempt to subdue the Plains tribes by wiping out their food source. Nonetheless, violent territorial disputes continued.

In the 1870s and 1880s, a religious movement called the Ghost Dance spread among the Plains tribes. The followers believed that if they

1

ceased violence against the whites and performed the Ghost Dance, the Great Spirit would disperse the white invaders from the tribes' land. Wovoka, the leader of the Ghost Dance movement, told the followers that wearing ghost shirts decorated with spiritual symbols would make them invincible to white men's bullets.

In 1876, Chief Sitting Bull and the Sioux nation successfully defeated Lieutenant Colonel George Armstrong Custer's troops at the Battle of Little Bighorn. When Sitting Bull, joined the Ghost Dance movement, the U.S. government became fearful of another uprising. In 1890, Sitting Bull was killed during an arrest attempt. The Sioux fled for the Badlands and the Black Hills of South Dakota. The U.S. government ordered the Sioux to return to the reservation, and a detachment of the U.S. Calvary intercepted them at Wounded Knee Creek.

While the soldiers were searching the Sioux camp for weapons, they observed a Ghost Dance and became unsettled. Lieutenant James D. Mann, an eyewitness of the event, noted that the troops saw a medicine man inside a semicircle of warriors. Tension escalated to gunshots and the deaths of 31 soldiers and over 100 Sioux. The ghost shirts' alleged ability to protect the wearers was disproven. The Battle of

"Ghost Dance of the Sioux Indians in North America." Courtesy of Library of Congress (LC-USZ62-52423 DLC).

Wounded Knee debunked the power of the Ghost Dance, quelled the Plains tribes' hope that the white invaders would leave, and marked an end to Native American resistance regarding westward expansion (Giordano 2007, 1:237–238).

When Native Americans posed less of a threat, exhibition shows such as Buffalo Bill's Wild West, and snake oil medicine shows with quack doctors, hired Native Americans to play the roles of war-thirsty savages and spiritual natural healers. For decades to follow, these Native American stereotypes were revisited in cowboy western literature, pulp magazines, comic books, films, movies, and television shows about the Wild West. Because of such cultural influences, the children's game Cowboys and Indians was popular well into the 20th century.

Native Americans as Savages

From about 1902 to 1934, the U.S. government strongly discouraged Native Americans from practicing their traditional ways of life in order to escalate their path from savagery to civilization (Chujoy 1949, 10; Needham 2002, 18). The idea of the savage originated when Europeans sought to explain cultural differences and justify their dominance over foreign peoples during the European colonial era (approximately 1500 to 1950). In the European imagination, "savage" became synonymous with a "painted and bizarrely costumed bodies, drumming and dancing with wild abandon by the light of a fire" (Ehrenreich 2006, 1).

The government's suppression of Native American cultures occurred during the Progressive era (1890s–1920s), a period of intense social reformation where a significant initiative was to civilize so-called lesser races. The notion of racial inequality was supported by popular 19th century evolutionary theories suggesting that all human races were at different places along the same ladder from savagery to civilization. Europeans supposedly were the most advanced on this ladder, and it was their responsibility to help the inferior races progress.

In 1901–1902, the Office of Indian Affairs of the U.S. Department of the Interior developed a list of Native American customs to be modified or discontinued. The list encouraged the cutting of braids, the cessation of skin painting (supposedly for health reasons), and the substitution of "Indian costume and blanket" for "citizens' clothing"

(Needham 2002, 36). The proposal explicitly stated, "Indian dances and so-called Indian feasts should be prohibited. In many cases these dances and feasts are simply subterfuges to cover degrading acts and to disguise immoral purposes" (Needham 2002, 36). Antidance regulations did not always prevent Native Americans from practicing their rituals, but they did encourage Native Americans to keep many of their rituals out of public view. Native Americans also adapted some rituals to conform to Christian worship, so that these rituals no longer would be perceived as primitive and savage.

Playing Indian

In the early 20th century, Native American dance forms were not easily accessible. Most schoolteachers who taught folk dance knew little about real Native American dance forms. Usually, if schoolteachers wanted to include Native American dances in their curricula, they composed character dances that tried to capture the essence of Native Americans. The dances needed only to have "lots of action," with tom-toms, bows and arrows, and peace pipes (Shafter 1927, 3).

Outside of schools, recreational youth groups with strong connections to nature also found inspiration in Native American imagery. Ernest Thompson Seton, founder of Woodcraft Indians (1902), an organization for non–Native American boys, and chairman of the founding committee of Boy Scouts of America (1910), helped introduce Native American references into youth camp culture (Smith 2002). Lois Postel, president of Phoenix International Folk Dancers, remembered that in the 1940s, her Camp Fire Girls of America group chose Native American nicknames, wore beaded ceremonial gowns beaded their own badges, carved totem poles, and improvised Native American dances around camp fires (interview by author, January 6, 2009).

As Native Americans left reservations to pursue mainstream lifestyles, some white Americans became concerned that Native American cultures would disappear. This was a pretext for the Smoki tribe of Prescott, Arizona, an all-white exhibition group whose members painted themselves a dark skin tone and imitated Native Americans in their annual Indian Ceremonials and Smoki Snake Dance (originally the Way Out West Show). The show began in 1921 as a way to raise money for the town's rodeo. The Smoki collected their dances from anthropologists who had visited reservations and from tribes who were willing to share their dances with outsiders. The show ended in 1990, in part because of Hopi protests against cultural exploitation and defacement of their rituals for entertainment (Leonard 2009).

Race-based evolution theories lost favor in the 1940s, replaced by anthropologist Franz Boas's theory of cultural relativism, which suggested that all cultural groups evolved independently and were best studied from the insiders' point of view. In addition to promoting self-representation among marginalized groups, Boas wrote about dance as a facet of culture. In doing so, he helped validate dance research as a serious topic of inquiry within the social sciences (Vissicaro 2004, 14). A short time later, dance anthropologists such as Gertrude Kurath, who laid the foundation for dance anthropology in 1960, studied Native American dance forms not for entertainment purposes, but instead to learn about their cultural significance and to accurately describe them from the insiders' point of view.

The civil rights movement, which peaked between 1955 and 1965, supported dance anthropologists' desire to more sensitively represent Native Americans. The movement also encouraged Native Americans to have pride in their heritage and to celebrate through intertribal events such as powwows. Many Native Americans relocated to reservations, wore traditional attire, ate traditional foods, studied disappearing languages, and revived almost-forgotten dance rituals. They created exhibition groups and competition teams not only to renew interest in these traditions among younger generations but also to educate and entertain the public while benefiting economically. After decades of exploitation by the entertainment industry, Native Americans finally determined how they wanted to represent themselves.

Native American Encounters

Places for cultural outsiders to observe Native American dances include folk festivals, powwows, and events on reservations that are open to the public. For instance, visitors can see dance performances year-round at the 19 Pueblos of New Mexico (Indian Pueblo Cultural Center, n.d.). Usually though, the most sacred rituals are kept out of public view in order to prevent cultural outsiders from exploiting the rituals for their own commercial interest. For this same reason, and to keep modern influences out of traditions, many tribes do not allow rituals to be photographed or videotaped.

Moontee Sinquah performs a Hoop Dance while his sons, Scott and Sampson, drum and sing. Phoenix Folkdance Festival, March 6, 2010. Courtesy of Michael S. Droz.

Moontee Sinquah of the Hopi tribe organizes Hoop Dance workshops for Native American children, competes in Hoop Dance competitions, and demonstrates Hoop Dance at festivals in different countries. Hoop Dance is a style of storytelling for which the dancer weaves in and out of multiple hoops to create shapes such as birds, butterflies, and reptiles. Outside of Native American communities, Sinquah observes that people are more interested in watching him perform than in learning the Hoop Dance themselves (interview by author, March 6, 2010).

Few cultural outsiders participate in Native American dance forms. An exception is the Hawaiian Hula, transformed from a ritual into a performance art for tourism and the movie industry in the 19th and 20th centuries. In the 1970s, shortly after Hawaii entered statehood, a Hawaiian cultural renaissance sought to revitalize traditional Hawaiian culture. The number of Hula schools teaching the traditional type of Hula increased in Hawaii and other states, welcoming people of all backgrounds. The opportunity to perform Hula onstage attracts many people to the dance form, but many people also enjoy Hula as a type of recreation (Susan Droz, interview by author, March 7, 2009; Cohen 2004, 3:394–396).

Today, recreational folk dance enthusiasts are likely to attend Native American dance workshops and festivals, and once in a while they adopt Native American venues into their own recreational practices. For instance, in Tucson, Arizona, folk dance teacher Andrew Carnie learned four dances at the Tohono O'odham's Waila Festival and taught them to his Lighthouse Folkdance Club. Each year, the Lighthouse Folkdance Club revisits the dances before the festival in order to participate. Three of the dances, called the Waila, the Chote, and the Mazurka, evolved from the Polka, the Schottische, and the Mazurka couple dances of 19th-century European ballrooms (see chapter 3). The other dance, Cumbia, consists of forward step-touches in line formations resembling the spokes of a wheel, and probably came from intertribal powwows (Andrew Carnie, e-mail to author, May 28, 2010).

Some people believe that Native American dances are the only true folk dances of America (Duggan, Schlottmann, and Rutledge 1948, 38). Ironically, Native American representation in the folk dance movement has been minimal. At first, the majority of Native American dances taught to schoolchildren were teacher-composed dances based on stereotypes. When recreational folk dance clubs for adults began in the 1930s and 1940s, Native American dances forms continued to be overlooked. The large-scale dismissal of Native American dance forms within the folk dance movement stems from Progressive era ideas that situate non-European groups as inferior to Europeans, and the widespread recognition of European dance forms as the most valuable folk dances.

2

African American Dances

Sub-Saharan Africans had highly developed dance forms that were meaningfully integrated into their lives long before the transatlantic slave trade began in the 16th century. Similar to the Native American dance forms, African dance forms symbolized the tribes' kinship with the Earth and spanned a range of themes including war, animal hunt, harvest, fertility, courtship, marriage, childbirth, rite of passage into adolescence or adulthood, healing, and death. The attributes of African dance forms varied widely across the continent. In North America, the term "African dance" usually refers to West African dance, the region from which most New World–bound slaves were uprooted (Cohen 2004, 6:382–383; Knowles 2002, 22).

In West Africa, dancers characteristically improvised and competed with one another inside of a circle of musicians and onlookers who clapped, stamped, and sang. Through music and dance, West Africans were able to reach a state of spiritual possession or trance and move into their ancestors' world. The dancers glided and shuffled using bent knees and bare feet. They hinged forward from the waist and moved outward from their pelvis in a loose manner. Movement patterns were polyrhythmic, meaning that the dancers' body parts expressed different rhythms simultaneously (Knowles 2002, 23–24).

West African dancers sometimes used playful mockery, derision, parody, satire, and humor to make social commentaries. Some gestures were intentionally sexual depending on the purpose of the dance, but the dancers did not consider displays of sexuality to be obscene. In fact, in some cases, overt sexuality facilitated spiritual possession by hastening a dancer's externalization and redirection of energy (Dunham 1983, 53). West Africans valued control, nonchalance, and composure. They demonstrated these virtues in their own ways, such as avoiding physical contact with others. Furthermore, West Africans danced for feeling more than appearance (Knowles 2002, 24).

Europeans, in contrast, characteristically danced with erect torsos, stepped smoothly and gracefully to even-metered choreographed patterns, and deemphasized the pelvis by keeping it in line with the upper body. Europeans commonly perceived West Africans dance forms as wild and licentious, full of hip swinging, pelvis thrusting, breast bouncing, and spear throwing. The notion that West African dance forms were savage suggested that West Africans were inferior to Europeans, even less than human, and provided support for the transatlantic slave trade. Colonial administrators in West Africa imposed bans on West African dancing in order to reduce uprisings, which were attributed to war dances. Some Christian missionaries also tried to eliminate West African dancing because of its strong religious significance (Cohen 2004, 6:382).

West African Dancing in the New World

An estimated 10 million West African slaves were brought to the New World. The majority of slaves disembarked in the West Indies, where they sometimes were seasoned on plantations for a few years in preparation for work farther north. In South America, Mexico, and Louisiana, Catholic missionaries allowed slaves to continue their music and dance traditions with certain restrictions. Missionaries also permitted the adoption of West African deities and customs into Christian worship. West African cultural influence was much stronger in these areas than in the English Protestant regions along the Atlantic coast. Protestants generally viewed slaves as nonhumans and were less tolerant of traditions that seemed to stand in the way of civilizing the so-called savages (Emery 1988, 15–16).

As slaves were moved around, they encountered other tribes, and dance forms such as the Calenda (from Guinea) gained intertribal appeal. The Calenda (sometimes the Calinda, the Kalenda, or the Jo-and-Johnny, among other names) involved one or more couples who interacted while encircled by onlookers who clapped and sang. The dancers faced one another and advanced and retreated as they shuffled, stamped, jumped, and turned. In at least one version of the Calenda observed in the 17th century, the dancers also striked their thighs together, locked arms, spun, and kissed. Europeans prohibited this dance form because they considered it offensive and distracting, because slaves did the dance for hours at a time. Nonetheless, slaves practiced the Calenda secretly into the 19th century. The Calenda may have influenced the following 20th century dance forms: the Black Bottom, the Charleston, the Foxtrot, and the Shimmy (Emery 1988, 21–24; Knowles 2002, 29).

New World authorities banned drums, horns, and loud music in fear that such sounds would provoke a slave uprising. Their fears were well founded, because drums were able to reproduce some West African dialects and send messages from one plantation to another. Music and dance regulations intensified after 1739, when a slave nick-named Cato led a rebellion that took the lives of several slaves and 25 whites in South Carolina. The rebellion was suppressed during a music and dance celebration to attract more slaves to join. When drums were banned on plantations, slaves used other types of instruments, their voices, and their bodies to create rhythmic accompaniment for dancing.

Slaves were known to have dance frolics on Saturday nights, which was usually their only time for recreation. They also danced at weddings, funerals, corn shuckings, quilting bees, and harvests, as well as for Christmas and Easter. Usually, a slave fiddler, whose job was to entertain, whites in the plantation's big house accompanied the dances in the slave quarters. Other popular instruments in the slave quarters included banjos (derived from a West African instrument), tambourines, quills or panpipes, animal jawbones played with a stick, and drums made from hollowed logs covered with animal hides, or kitchen pots and pans (Emery 1988, 86–87, 103).

Slave owners generally learned to dance from dancing masters and dance manuals. Slaves, on the other hand, did not have access to dancing masters, and most slaves could not read manuals. Slave fiddlers learned popular European dances while playing for parties in the big house. The fiddlers then went to the slave quarters and taught the European dances to other slaves. This is quite possibly the origin of the caller in American Square Dance, according to Phil Jamison, dance

Winter Holidays in the Southern States: Plantation Frolic on Christmas Eve, 1857 (wood engraving). Courtesy of Library of Congress (LC-USZ62-49657).

historian and coordinator of Warren Wilson College's Appalachian Music Program (e-mail to author, May 16, 2010).

Early African American Dances and Blackface Minstrelsy

The transatlantic slave trade ended in 1807, reducing the amount of cultural influence directly from West Africa. Around the same time, an evangelical religious movement called the Great Awakening swept over North America, and many African Americans converted to Baptism and Methodism. These denominations encouraged experiential worship and were adaptable to African rituals, but they condemned secular dancing as sinful. Social dancing declined on some plantations and new dance forms such as the Ring Shout developed within African American Baptist churches (Knowles 2002, 56, 59).

The Ring Shout (also called the Running Sperichils) may have evolved from the BaKongo practice of dancing over geometric figures drawn on the ground in order to evoke spirits. For this dance, a song leader gave directions to the dancers while a stickman beat a broom against the floor, and a chorus of singers answered the phrases called out by the leader. The dancers traveled in a circle using flat-footed shuffling steps, clapped their hands, and waved their arms. Sometimes they reached a state of spiritual possession. Baptists never crossed feet, however, because they associated crossed feet with secular dancing (Knowles 2002, 59–61).

In areas less impacted by the Great Awakening, solo step dances were common among African Americans and poor whites. The dances went by a variety of names, including Buck Dance, Buck and Wing, Pigeon Wing, Jig, Hoedown, Flat-footing, Sure-footing, and Shuffling. "Buck Dance," the most widespread term, could refer to any solo step dance. The term "Buck" came from the West Indies, where slaves used "Po' Bockorau" in reference to a troublesome sailor or buccaneer. Slaves in North America shortened "Po' Bockorau" to "Po Buck" to describe the poor Irish immigrants in the Carolinas and re-named the Irish Jig as Buck (Duke 1984, 27; Knowles 2002, 40–42).

After 1939, southern Appalachian step dance forms became known as Clogging (or Clog Dance) after a similar English dance form with the same name (Duke 1984, 21). Southern Appalachian Clogging is considered a type of American folk dance. It has roots in European, West African, and possibly Native American dance forms. Minimal documentation existed on southern Appalachian step dances before the 20th century. This was because the dances were largely improvisatory, and sometimes the people who did the dances were illiterate. Furthermore, city trendsetters generally perceived these dances as unsophisticated. With such a reputation, step dances easily migrated into blackface minstrelsy.

Blackface minstrelsy was a form of comedy show that severely degraded the image of African Americans. The early artists were white and took inspiration from African American, Irish, and English sources. They used burnt cork to darken their faces and exaggerated their lips for comical effect. In 1828, Tom Rice performed as Jim Crow, a poorly educated and childish slave who did a shuffling dance. Later, George Washington Dixon performed as Zip Coon (sometimes Jim Dandy), a lazy and unreliable city dandy whose song "Zip Coon" later was renamed "Turkey in the Straw." Jim Crow and Zip Coon became two of the most popular characters in blackface minstrelsy (Knowles 2002, 77, 86).

In 1840, a 17-year-old performer named John (sometimes Johnny or Jack) Diamond gained acclaim as one of the best solo dancers in the industry. A year later, however, he extorted money from his manager, P. T. Barnum, and was replaced by a free-born African American named William Henry Lane, who was billed as Master Juba, the Dancing Wonder of the Age. Lane developed his own Jig style that was an early form of Tap Dance. He also successfully imitated other Jig dancers of the day, including his rival, Diamond. In 1944, the two performers participated in a series of challenge dances to determine the best dancer. Lane won the competition and gained the title King of All Dancers (Knowles 2002, 88–91).

Lane's success helped pave the way for African Americans in the entertainment industry. The first African American minstrel troupes appeared in the mid-1850s, but permanent troupes did not exist until after the Civil War (1861–1865). Ironically, the African American performers were restricted in how much they could modify the degrading caricatures. They continued to darken their skin with burnt cork, following the tradition. Over time, however, African American performers began to reshape minstrel dances, stripping them of unrealistic and grotesque qualities. They also introduced new dance forms such as Stop-Time Tapping (Knowles 2002, 118).

Blackface entertainers experimented with different types of shoes and dance styles in attempt to stand out from other performers. By the 1910s, two step dance forms dominated: the Buck and Wing, with wooden-soled shoes, and the Soft Shoe, with leather-soled shoes. The Buck and Wing evolved from the Buck Dance and the Pigeon Wing, a plantation dance in which the footwork resembled a pigeon flapping its wings. The Soft Shoe evolved from the Essence of Old Virginia (also called the Essence, the Essence of Virginia, or the Virginia Essence), a loose, casual step dance perfected by minstrel performer Dan Bryant in the 1850s. The Essence of Old Virginia, in turn, probably came from a step dance style in southern Appalachia region (Emery 1988, 193). By the late 1920s, Buck and Wing and the Soft Shoe merged into Tap Dance, with metal plates or taps added to leather soles to accentuate the sounds (Duggan 1936, viii).

The Cakewalk, the Tango, Ragtime Dances, Jazz Dances, and the Jitterbug

The first African American dance to achieve popularity among whites in social settings was the Cakewalk (also the Chalk Line Walk, among other names). The Cakewalk was a plantation dance that involved strutting in imitation of wealthy whites at formal balls. Cakewalk competitions were held for white audiences where the winning couple received a cake, thus the expression "take the cake." The Cakewalk appeared on Broadway in 1885, gained international acclaim, and was a fad dance in wealthy ballrooms into the early 1900s (Knowles 2002, 44–46; Giordano 2007, 1:259–261).

A Tango craze occurred about a decade after whites embraced the Cakewalk. The Tango originated in the slums of Argentina and traveled to Paris in 1910, where it was refined by dancing masters before coming to the United States in 1911. In 1912, cafés held *dansants,* or tango teas, that catered to the working class but attracted participants from

Primrose & West's Big Minstrels, circa 1896. Courtesy of Library of Congress, Minstrel Poster Collection (LC-USZC2-1773).

all social backgrounds. The physical proximity of partners, the sex-
ually suggestive movement, and the mixing of classes created a stir.
Importantly, the Tango triggered a dance mania that emphasized rhythmic improvisation, moving the body to the tune of the music, rather
than strictly following pre-choreographed steps (Walkowitz 2010,
57–58).

The popularity of the Cakewalk and Tango sparked interest in African American social dance forms as material for cabarets, Broadway
performances, and vaudeville shows. Directors borrowed African
American dance forms from nightclubs and dance halls and modified
them for the stage. From the stage, then, the modified versions of the
dances often made their way into white dance halls. In order to keep
up with the short-lived fads, some whites went directly to the source
to observe how African Americans were dancing.

In low-income areas, African American nightclubs and dance halls
were known as jook joints, honky-tonks, and after-hours joints
(Knowles 2002, 68). These places had a reputation for rowdiness and
sinful behavior. It was in such places that myriad African American
dance forms developed to the syncopated sounds of ragtime music.
When ragtime dances entered white dance halls, however, polite society (the upper class) showed a great deal of resistance. These dance
forms could not shake the reputation of the places in which they had
originated.

Unlike the group and solo dances that had been popular on plantations, the ragtime dances were designed for male-female couples. The most infamous ragtime dances were the animal dances,
which included the Turkey Trot, the Bunny Hug, and the Grizzly Bear.
In *Dancing Made Easy* (1919), Charles J. Coll described these dances as
"an orgy of perversion," "acrobatic bedlam," and "fearsome things."
He also explained why these dances were popular: "It was something
the people had wanted, and it gave them an outlet to that abandon
that had been pent up so long" (41).

When the animal dances arrived in white dance venues, they often replaced the Waltz, and Two-Step, the most popular turn-of-the-
century social dances in North America (Shaw 1949, 25; Castle 1958,
85–86). Simple and improvisatory in nature, the animal dances did
not require lessons. This frustrated dance teachers who made their living teaching dances that required choreographic memorization and

training in grace and precision. The animal dances upset moralists to such an extent that the Vatican formally denounced the Turkey Trot in 1914. The animal dances declined shortly thereafter, replaced by the One-Step and the newly invented Foxtrot.

The One-Step (also One Step) and the Turkey Trot were sometimes considered the same dance or close relatives (Coll 1919, 49). The One-Step that became popular after the animal dances, however, "eliminated all hoppings, all contortions of the body, all flouncing of the elbows, all twisting of the arms, and, above all else, all fantastic dips" (Castle 1914, 20). Vernon and Irene Castle, famous ballroom dancers of the early 20th century, condemned the Turkey Trot and were responsible for giving elegance to the One-Step. In their coauthored book titled *Modern Dancing* (1914), the Castles described the step pattern as follows: "The gentleman starts forward with his left foot, and the lady steps backward with her right, walking in time with the music. Bear in mind this one important point: When I say *walk,* that is all it is" (44).

The Foxtrot (also Fox Trot, Fox-trot, Horsetrot, or Fishwalk) may have originated from a 1913 vaudeville act in which a performer named Henry Fox alternated a slow walk with three trotting steps (Giordano 2007, 2:13–14). Coll credits Vernon Castle as the originator of the Foxtrot, stating,

> On one of [Castle's] quests for innovations his attention was called to a certain exclusive colored club. At the time he attended, the members were dancing the Fox Trot, even at that time so-called, and he became enthusiastic over it and determined to bring it out for a little fun for a few, hardly realizing that the dance was to win for itself a high place in the favor of the many. (1919, 46)

The Castles and other professional ballroom dancers regularly performed the Foxtrot and inspired people to flock to dance studios for instruction. In the 1920s, Arthur Murray included the Foxtrot in his mail-order footprint diagrams so that people could learn the dance from home. Murray also taught the Foxtrot through his New York City studio, which turned into a franchise in 1937. In short time, the Foxtrot became one of the most popular dances in North America, occurring in schools, ballrooms, and folk dance venues (Hall 1963, 196).

After the Foxtrot came a series of jazz dances including the Charleston and the Shimmy. In the late 1920s, jazz music quickened and inspired a new genre called swing dance. The Jitterbug, an acrobatic form of swing dance, ruled North American dance halls when recreational folk dance clubs began to spread in the 1940s. Some folk dancers perceived the Jitterbug as a rival to their own activity. In the June 1943 issue of the *Folk Dancer,* for instance, editor and folk dance leader Michael Herman suggested that young people were attracted to the Jitterbug because they wanted to release "physical and emotional tensions heightened by the fears and insecurity of war times." Herman believed that folk dancing was a better option, because, in his opinion, the Jitterbug served to "arouse and intensify emotions rather than to release them" (Herman 1943, 3).

Automobile manufacturer Henry Ford strongly opposed the African American dance fads that were gaining prevalence in the early 20th century. In response, Ford launched an old-fashioned dance revival from the 1920s through the 1940s mainly to revive white social dance forms, particularly the Quadrille. In *Good Morning: After a Sleep of Twenty-Five Years, Old-Fashioned Dancing Is Being Revived by Mr. and Mrs. Ford* (1926), the authors explained that the contemporary popular couple dances lacked the group spirit of fun (8). The Fords' nationwide promotion of white ballroom dances had the additional effect of augmenting public interest in rural American dance forms of European origin.

3

European Dances

Dancing was an integral part of life and education in ancient Greece (1100 BC–146 BC). In the early 20th century, when educators sought to justify the inclusion of dance into physical education programs, they often cited ancient Greece as an example of unparalleled achievement (Gulick 1910, 1). The ancient Romans (509 BC–AD 476) borrowed dance traditions from the Greeks for their own education and festivities. During the European Middle Ages (5th–15th centuries), however, the importance of dance in education declined as ritual dancing lost favor in Christian worship.

Ritual dancing enabled people to access deities on their own through ecstatic trance or self-abandonment. Early Christians, until the fourth century, followed the Jewish practice of performing worship as a drama or dance, with repetitive circling of the altar. As Christianity spread (usually underground) to other cultures, local pagan ceremonies became incorporated into worship. In the fourth century, when Constantine made Christianity the official religion of the Roman Empire, the church became more structured and powerful. Whereas the early church worshiped literally underground, the Roman Church built edifices above ground, usually in round shapes to facilitate processional dancing around the baptismal font. Gradually, the church began to regulate the ecstatic nature of ritual dancing. By preventing trance, the church could be the sole mediator between the laity and God. Nonetheless, ecstatic dancing at church continued (Ehrenreich 2006, 64–65, 73, 83–84).

By the 12th and 13th centuries, church authorities recognized the need for alternative celebratory outlets. Their solution was to allow the laity to celebrate however they wished on Christian holidays, so long as these celebrations occurred outside of churches. Many historians perceive the sudden growth of festivities in the 12th and 13th centuries as an inexplicable surge in creativity, but historian Barbara Ehrenreich suggests that these festivities always existed; they merely changed venue. Over time, the church distanced itself from its own holidays, so that religious rituals joined the realm of secular festivities, done for the people's own communal pleasure (Ehrenreich 2006, 64–77, 79, 93).

Rapid population growth in 16th-century Europe caused prices to rise and wages to fall. Thousands of displaced people wandered the countryside begging and stealing or moved to cities as the new urban underclass. Public festivities such as Carnival, where all social classes attended and masks concealed individuals' faces, provided the perfect opportunity for people to express frustration through violence and rebellion. It was under these conditions that Europe became the birthplace of Protestantism, a branch of Christianity that declared public festivities sinful and vulgar and convinced large numbers of people that their lives should be spent on disciplined labor and worship. Protestant leader Martin Luther tried to abolish superstitious saint-day celebrations, but he did not consider social fun itself evil. John Calvin, on the other hand, condemned all forms of festive behavior and leisure activities, particularly dancing, drinking, gambling, and sports (Ehrenreich 2006, 101, 104–105).

Shortly after Protestantism appeared, firearms spread throughout Europe and replaced bows and arrows, swords, and other weapons. Peasants began to use firearms in their rebellions, which overlapped with festivities that often featured shooting contests. The upper class grew increasingly wary of attending these events and began to hold their own parallel festivities. Kings, however, were not comfortable with their subordinates shooting, dueling, or engaging in other forms of violence. The upper class was required to reside at the royal court several months per year and learn manners. In courts, notions of personal space and self-restraint cultivated through manners gradually replaced the idea of communal existence. To the aristocracy, group ecstasy became something that lower-class Europeans or savages experienced (Ehrenreich 2006, 9, 116).

Life in the royal courts influenced social activities and fashions throughout Europe. During the European Renaissance (15th–16th centuries), music, poetry, drama, philosophy, painting, architecture, and astronomy thrived in courts in a way that had not happened since antiquity. Dance in education reappeared. The earliest known dance manual for urban use was *L'art et instruction de bien dancer* (circa 1488) by an anonymous author in Paris. Other manuals appeared soon after in England, Germany, and Italy. The number of dancing masters increased in the late 16th century, around the time a monk named Jehan Tabourot helped reintroduce dancing as part of church ceremony in France and wrote a popular manual on French court dance titled *Orchésographie* (1588), using the pseudonym Thoinot Arbeau (Cohen 2004, 2:338–339; Giordano 2007, 1:21).

Most 17th-century European court dances evolved from English, French, German, Italian, and Spanish peasant dances. Dancing masters refined peasant dances by adding bows, curtseys, and fancy footwork such as *assemblés, balancés, balotés, chassés, coupés, emboîts,* glissades, jetés, pas de basques, rigadoons, and *sissones* (Richardson 1960, 62). Before the 17th century, dancing masters were fencing instructors who taught dance in order to improve their pupils' grace and balance for sword handling. By the 17th century, however, the prestigious art of ballet had spread throughout the royal courts, validated the importance of dance training, and redefined the role of dancing master as a dance specialist. Aristocrats and members of the upper class flocked to dancing masters to learn the popular social dances, perfect the stylized balletic footwork, and refine their manners (Cohen 2004, 2:338).

For most of the 17th century, European balls featured some group dances and several ceremonial or presentational couple dances where one or two couples danced at a time and everyone else carefully observed them. For the most part, dance partners only made physical contact with their hands, and they maintained a modest distance of an arm's length. The dances typically shared names with their accompanying musical forms, such as Allemande, Bourrée, Branle, Courante, Gavotte, Gigue, Minuet, Passepied, Rigadoon, and Sarabande. The balls featured orchestras with several types of instruments, including flutes, tambourines, and an early form of violin that usually carried the tune for the dance. As for clothing style, the men wore buckled shoes, stockings, britches, a puffy shirt with long lace cuffs, and a bright knee-length coat. The women wore high-heeled shoes, floor-length hooped

French Ball, circa 1660. An engraving by Abraham Rosse in Lilly Grove's *Dancing* (1907), page 249. Courtesy of Library of Congress (GV1601 F84 1907, Digital ID musdi 077 http://hdl.loc.gov/loc.music/musdi.077).

dresses, three-quarter-length sleeves, a low-cut collar, and jewelry. For both sexes, the outfits were topped off with large powdered wigs, hats, and headdresses (Giordano 2007, 1:29).

Dancing in the American Colonies

Large-scale migration from northwestern Europe to North America began in the late 16th century. In the 17th and 18th centuries, 13 British colonies were established along the east coast of what became the United States of America. Most colonists came from the British Isles, France, Germany, and Scandinavia. By 1700, the population of the colonies was about 250,000. Another 5,000 people lived in areas controlled by Spain, which included Florida and most of the Southwest. The French areas had a population of about 15,000 concentrated in settlements along the St. Lawrence River and the Mississippi River (Giordano 2007, 1:4).

In 1607, a group of entrepreneurs called the Virginia Company established the first successful British settlement in Jamestown with the objective of economic prosperity. These settlers brought music and dance knowledge from their homeland, but there is little evidence of how or when they danced. Most likely, their time was spent on survival tasks and coping with disease, famine, and indigenous raids. When agriculture proved profitable in Virginia, the British founded more colonies in what are now Maryland, the Carolinas, and Georgia. In 1664, they seized the port of New Amsterdam from the Dutch and expanded into what are now New York, New Jersey, Pennsylvania, and Delaware.

In 1620, a group of Puritans bound for Virginia fell off course and landed in Plymouth in present-day Massachusetts. Their success over the next decade inspired approximately 20,000 Puritans to settle in New England between 1630 and 1640. The Puritans aimed to eliminate all Catholic influence from within the Church of England. They perceived the New World as a utopia where they could practice religion based on their own terms. They believed in a strict interpretation of the Bible, the absolute sovereignty of God, and the authority of religious leaders in political matters. New England branched out from Massachusetts to encompass Connecticut, Maine, New Hampshire, Rhode Island, and Vermont.

New England religious authorities prohibited drama, games, gambling, dancing, drinking, feasting, and other secular forms of amusement believed to distract people from their religious obligations. They also forbade anything related to paganism such as maypole dances, which had been part of English tradition for hundreds of years. In 1684, a 30-page discourse titled *An Arrow Against Profane and Promiscuous Dancing Drawn Out of the Quiver of Scriptures,* most likely written by a Boston minister named Increase Mather, interpreted several biblical references to show that dancing was a vicious practice and evil. Still, 17th-century court records indicate that New Englanders continued to dance even at the risk of being fined or going to hell. Puritan influence on New England social life declined after the 1689 Glorious Revolution in England which marked the end of the Puritan theocracy. By 1700, many New Englanders had incorporated social dancing into their lives (Giordano 2007, 1:42–51).

In the mid-Atlantic colonies, which were not governed by Puritan ministers, dancing was a popular form of recreation except on the Sabbath. On plantations, slaves and white indentured servants practiced their own dance forms and imitated the social elite's dances. When plantation owners became wealthy with cash crops supported by inexpensive labor, they looked to Europe for fashionable leisure activities to fill their time. They consulted books such as Richard Brathwaite's *The English Gentleman* (1630) and *The English Gentle-woman* (1631), which endorsed dance training as part of a proper education (Giordano 2007, 1:54).

Many plantation libraries included books specifically about dancing, such as Pierre Rameau's *Le Maître à danser* (1725), translated into English by John Essex as *The Dancing-Master; or, The Art of Dancing Explained* (1728). This book described dance positions, figures, and the social customs of a ball at the royal court of King Louis XIV. Another popular book was Kellom Tomlinson's *The Art of Dancing* (1735), about French dances and written for English readers. The French royal court was a leading cultural authority, and it strongly influenced social customs and dance practices throughout Europe and the American colonies, especially on plantations (Giordano 2007, 1:27, 30–34; Richardson 1960, 19, 40).

English Country Dance, Contradanse Française, and the Cotillon

A new dance form swept over Europe in the late 17th century. Originating among English peasants, it became known as English Country Dance. Early records of English Country Dance indicate that it was danced at the royal court of Queen Elizabeth I, who reigned from 1558 to 1603. English Country Dance continued under King James I and King Charles I. The degree to which Oliver Cromwell, ruler of the Commonwealth of England, accepted these dances is unclear. During his brief rule from 1649 to 1658, the Puritans ordered the closure of all London theaters and the removal of musical instruments from churches. Cromwell's daughter had dancing at her wedding, however, and dance historians believe that it was English Country Dance. With the monarchy restored under Charles II in 1660, English Country Dance reappeared in the royal court (Giordano 2007, 1:35).

An English publisher and musician named John Playford wrote the first known manual about English Country Dance, *The English Dancing-Master; or, Plaine and Easie Rules for the Dancing of Country Dances, with the Tune to Each Dance* (1651). The pocket-sized manual included over 100 descriptions of tunes and dances in circle, square, and parallel line or longways sets. The dances were named for accompanying tunes. The couple in the head position of the set, closest to the musicians,

English Country Dance from Lilly Grove's *Dancing* (1895). Author's archives.

started the dance. The lead lady usually called the tune. The original footwork for English Country Dance is unknown, but the dancers probably used a smooth, gliding walk (Richardson 1960, 48–49). Patri J. Pugliese explains the basic structure of an English Country Dance from Playford's era:

> The first part begins with all [couples] leading up and back, the second part with partners "siding" (approaching each other until they are side by side, and returning to places), and the third with partners "arming" (turning with arms joined). In some cases, the figure that follows the initial leading up and back is repeated as a refrain in the second and third parts. (Cohen 2004, 2:255)

These three characteristic parts of Playford dances came from popular continental European Renaissance dances, as Italian and French dancing masters often visited London (Walkowitz 2010, 47).

English Country Dance enabled any number of couples to participate in a dance, as long as they were able to find positions within a set. Several sets were on the dance floor at the same time. Ladies almost always stood to the right of their male partners. Square sets were made of either two couples or four couples, so that either one person or one couple stood on each side of an imaginary square. The circle sets and longways sets were either for a specific number of couples or for as many as will, meaning any number of couples could join the set. For longways sets, partners usually stood across from each other in facing lines. The following diagrams adapted from Playford's *The English Dancing-Master* (1651) illustrate some set possibilities.

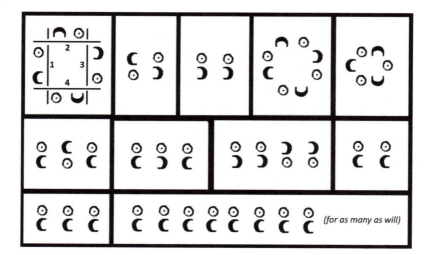

Formations for English Country Dance adapted from John Playford's *The English Dancing-Master* (1651). Author's archives.

A unique attribute of many English court dances was their progression. Each time through a dance sequence, all couples moved as pairs to a new position within the set to repeat the sequence. The longways dances usually were triple minors, meaning that the top three couples were a subset, the next three couples were another subset, and so on down the set. In each subset, the couple closest to the musicians was the active couple. They danced with the second and third couples, who were considered inactive or semi-active. The progression enabled the dancers to dance with everyone in the set and for the inactive couples eventually to become active (Walkowitz 2010, 43–44).

Longways dances, for any number of couples, substantially outnumbered other kinds of dances in later editions of *The Dancing Master* series (about 17 total). Longways dances were the most popular style of English Country Dance when the French adopted the dance form in the 1680s. The French translated English Country Dance as Danse Anglaise. In 1706, French dancing master Raoul-Auger Feuillet (creator of the Feuillet notation system, commissioned by King Louis XIV to record the court dances) only documented longways dances under the label Danse Anglaise (Cohen 2004, 2:254–255; Richardson 1960, 46).

In the 18th century, French dancing masters modified Danse Anglaise with the fancy balletic footwork of the French court and limited the number of dancers to two or four couples, creating a new dance form called Contradanse Française (also Contradanse or Contradance). The term *contradanse* most likely is a transliteration of the English term "country dance." Contradanse Française replaced Danse Anglaise at the French royal court, and the dance form spread throughout Europe and North America by way of French dance manuals and dancing masters (Cohen 2004, 5:285; Richardson 1960, 48–49).

Following Contradanse Française, a French peasant dance inspired another French court dance in square formation called the Cotillon (Anglicized as Cotillion). The Cotillon was a dance for two or four couples that probably evolved from a circle dance. *Cotillon* is translated as "underpetticoat." The name most likely came from the title and lyrics of a song to which the Cotillon was danced. Dance historian Desmond Strobel described the structure of a Cotillon as follows:

> A typical cotillon begins (after the usual honors [bows and curtseys]) with Le Grand Rond, a circular figure involving all eight dancers. Following this the figure proper begins; one couple dances with the couple standing opposite across the set. The remaining two couples then duplicate this maneuver. Next follows "the first change," or refrain, during which all four couples simultaneously turn their partners, first with the right hand and then with the left hand. The figure proper then repeated by the leading couples and the side couples, as before. Then "the second change" begins—usually a turn with both hands performed by all couples simultaneously. The figure is then repeated, always alternated with a different change, until ten changes have been danced. (Cohen 2004, 2:252)

Dance manuals sometimes confused the French-derived Cotillon and the English-derived Contradanse, because both used square formations. The Cotillon reached North America in the 1770s. By the end of the 18th century, nearly all European and North American ballrooms dedicated half of their programs to Contradanse and Cotillon. The Minuet, an elegant and intricate presentational couple dance, often made up the other half of the program. English Country Dance also was popular in English ballrooms (Richardson 1960, 35, 46–48).

The term "Cotillon," in reference to a square dance, was dropped by the 1840s. The term was readopted for a popular ballroom dance game that involved choosing partners, mixing up partners, accomplishing goals with props, and distributing party favors or gifts for winning a dance competition. After the American Civil War, the Cotillon dance game also was called the German. Dance manuals sometimes dedicated dozens of pages to the hundreds of Cotillon or German dance games. At formal balls, Cotillon or German dance games either occurred between dances or all together at the end of the evening (Giordano 2007, 1:242; Shaw 1949, 39).

Almack's Assembly Rooms, Scottish Dance, and Closed-Position Couple Dances

In 1765, Almack's Assembly Rooms, was established in London. It was a prestigious social club for which membership was nearly impossible to obtain. For the first half of the 19th century, the dances in fashion at Almack's were copied just about everywhere in Europe and North America (Richardson 1960, 30). Almack's was based on master of ceremonies Beau Nash's assembly room model at the Bath medicinal resort from the previous century. For an admission fee, Beau Nash allowed the public to participate in his ornate assembly room balls, which usually happened Tuesday and Wednesday evenings from 6 P.M. until 11 P.M., with breaks for tea and refreshments (Giordano 2007, 1:42).

In the late 18th century, Almack's featured French court dances, particularly the Minuet, Contradanse, and Cotillon, as well as English Country Dance. Furthermore, a wave of Scottish dances or Scottish-inspired dances passed through Almack's in the late 18th century and early 19th century. The most popular Scottish Country Dance was the Scottish Reel, an interweaving group dance with active and inactive couples, sequence repetition, and progression. The footwork for the Scottish Reel consisted of gliding steps and cross-steps punctuated with hops and leaps (Grove 1907, 192). A popular Scottish-inspired dance in was the Écossaise, which borrows figures from Scottish Reels and was done to Scottish music usually in 2/4 time.

The heightened interest in Scottish dance may be linked the repeal of the Act of Proscription in 1781. The act, instated by the Parliament of Great Britain in 1746 after a Scottish rebellion, attempted to suppress traditional Scottish practices such as wearing kilts and playing bagpipes. The repeal of the act, the fame of Sir Walter Scott's writings, and admiration for Scottish soldiers who had participated in the Napoleonic campaigns all enhanced the status of Scotland. Furthermore, at this time, Almack's was owned by a Scotsman and featured Neil

Gow's famous Scottish band (Richardson 1960, 52). London society's enthusiasm for Scottish Country Dance helped popularize this dance form in Scotland and England, but Scottish dances helped introduce these dances into British and North American ballrooms. But at Almack's, Scottish dances never were as popular as English Country Dance or the dance forms that came from Paris.

After the French Revolution of 1789, France continued to be an important influence on dance fashion, even though Europeans and Americans generally dismissed the presentational dance forms and clothing styles connected to the French aristocracy. An exception was the Minuet, which remained popular in Great Britain and the United States through the 1820s (Richardson 1960, 41). Rather than the French royal court, Europeans and Americans looked to ancient Greece and peasants for inspiration. Powdered wigs were discarded for natural hair. Slacks and vertical Grecian-style gowns replaced knickers and hoop skirts. Peasants' closed-position couple dances, previously thought to be unsophisticated, were refined by Parisian dancing masters and made their way into middle-class and upper-class dance venues. Nationalistic groups in foreign-occupied nations such as Bohemia (what is now the western part of the Czech Republic) also promoted peasant dances for nation-building purposes. Their efforts may have increased the popularity of such dances among sympathizers elsewhere in Europe and America (Richardson 1960, 17).

The Waltz was the first closed-position couple dance to enter European and American ballrooms. It probably originated from German peasants, who were known for similar dances, and arrived in Paris in 1795 as part of Pierre Gardel's ballet-pantomime *La Dansomanie.* London society danced the Waltz at Almack's as early as 1812, and the Waltz came to the United States in the 1830s. The dance form's characteristic face-to-face embrace was so revolutionary for its era that it became known as the Waltz position. Sometimes, other dance forms that used the same or a similar closed position were labeled as the Waltz. The Waltz was is done in 3/4 time, and the basic footwork consisted of six smooth steps where partners pivoted around one another or turned together. At first, polite society condemned the Waltz because it supposedly led to immoral behavior and poor health (Shaw 1949, 49, 104–105). In 1885, dancing master Allen Dodworth, described the Waltz as "the dance which has for fifty years resisted every kind of attack, and is to-day the most popular known" (1885, 62).

The proper way.   Extremely vulgar.

Proper and vulgar versions of the Waltz position from Allen Dodworth's *Dancing* (1885). Author's archives.

In the early 1800s, another closed-position dance called the Galop arrived in ballrooms, perhaps to give dancers relief from the dizzying Waltz (Shaw 1949, 114). The Galop may have evolved from a figure in the Quadrille, a popular 19th-century square dance. The Galop was done in 2/4 time and consisted of gallops or step-closes (also called *chassés*) in lines or zigzags across the room. Pivots and turns were used only to change directions after several measures of music. In the second half of the 19th century, another dance, the Galopade, appeared with only two steps to either side. The Galop and Galopade were popular in American ballrooms from the 1830s through the 1890s (Giordano 2007, 1:153–155).

The Polka most likely originated in Bohemia in the 1830s. A popular origination story suggests that a peasant girl named Anna joyously danced the Polka by herself to a tune in her head. By the 1840s, prejudices against closed-position couple dances had diminished, and a Polka mania rapidly swept over European and American ballrooms. Parisian dancing masters Cellarius, Coralli, Laborde, and Petipa were the Polka's main exponents (Richardson 1960, 83). Dance historian Lloyd Shaw described the basic Polka step pattern as hop-step-close-step twice, alternating feet, in 2/4 time. In some areas of the United States, the hop was omitted for a more grounded side heel click (Shaw 1949, 72–73).

The Polish Mazurka, riding on the Polka's success, entered European ballrooms next. The Mazurka used four basic steps in 3/4 time with leaps, stamps, and glides. In addition to these steps, according to Cellarius, "the rest [was] invented, [was] extemporized, in the excitement of execution." Cellarius also mentioned that a promenade, "executed by holding the lady by the right hand and making her perform a course," was "indispensible, before each figure" (1847, 52–55). The Mazurka was too difficult to gain widespread acceptance in its original form in the United States. Part of the confusion may have been because the dance began on the last beat of a measure (Shaw 1949, 118, 247). However, Mazurka steps were used to create hybrid dances including Mazurka Quadrilles, Mazurka Waltzes, and Polka-Mazurkas (Giordano 2007, 1:174–175).

The Redowa was a Waltz-like dance that may have originated from a Mazurka Quadrille around 1847. The foundation of the Redowa was the Polish Pas de Basque in 3/4 time, one of the four basic Mazurka steps. Shaw described the Pas de Basque from the gentleman's point of view as follows: "Stand on your left foot with your right in front. Swing your right out, around and behind your left and, stepping on your right in this backward crossed position, at the same time lift the left off the floor" (1949, 240). The step then repeated with the left foot leading. The Redowa also inspired hybrid dances such as the Polka Redowa in 3/4 time, and it was the forerunner of the 20th-century Waltz (Giordano 2007, 1:175–176).

In the 1850s, the Varsovienne (sometimes called the Varsouvianna) combined steps from the Mazurka, Polka, or Polka-Mazurka. Shaw explained,

The characteristic steps for the Varsouvianna are first, a sweep back of the foot, second a glide forward on the foot and third a close of the other foot to it. This sweep-glide-close is to the dancer a series of three steps or a measure; but actually the sweep comes on the last beat of one measure, and the glide and close on the first two beats of the next measure. (1949, 247)

The name of the dance probably referred to the city of Warsaw in Poland, but it is unclear whether the dance originated there or whether it simply had the characteristics of a Polish dance. In Texas, the dance was known as Little Foot or Put Your Little Foot after an accompanying song. In other parts of the United States, the Varsovienne also was called See My New Shoes (Shaw 1949, 245–246).

Around the same time the Varsovienne entered North American ballrooms, the Schottische (sometimes the Schottisch) was gaining momentum. In German, *Schottische* means "Scottish." The Schottische may have originated from the Bavarian Polka (also known as the Rheinlaender), or from the Écossaise. The basic step pattern for the Schottische consisted of step-close-step-hop twice, leading with each foot, followed by four step-hops in a circle. Before the 1890s, dancers did the entire Schottische sequence in closed position. Then, a variation of the Schottische popularized the side-by-side or open position for the first part of the sequence, and only the step-close-step-hops were done in closed position (Richardson 1960, 53–54; Shaw 1949, 270–272).

The Quadrille and Prompters

In the early 19th century, French dancing masters combined popular Contradanse and Cotillon figures, resulting in a new dance form called the Quadrille. The Quadrille was an essential part of European and American ballroom programs for most of the 19th century. The name may have originated from a card game in which four people sat at the sides of a table. Other sources trace the term to a horseback military exercise in square formation (Richardson 1960, 59). Thomas Wilson's *Quadrille and Cotillon Panorama* (1822) indicated that the early Quadrilles incorporated the fancy footwork of the French court dances, but dance historian Philip Richardson believed that "these difficult steps were only used by a few accomplished dancers who wished to 'show off'"

(1960, 62). By the 1840s, dancers did the Quadrille with smooth gliding steps, on par with the Waltz and other contemporaneous ballroom dances (Cohen 2004, 5:286).

The Quadrille consisted of two head couples (Couple 1 and Couple 2) and two side couples (Couple 3 and Couple 4), all facing the middle of an imaginary square. Couple 1 stood with backs toward the musicians and Couple 2 faced Couple 1, looking at the musicians. Couple 3 stood to the right of Couple 1, and Couple 4 stood opposite of Couple 3. Margot Mayo, former leader of the American Square Dance Group, in New York City, explained the structure of a Quadrille as follows:

> In the traditional quadrille, the couples become active in turn which amounts to each figure being repeated four times. As each figure has its own music, frequently, with a change of tempo and mood, it is customary to wait for eight measures of music to be played at the beginning of each figure in order to "get the feel" of the music. The only exception to this rule is at the end of the last figure when a chord is played as an introduction for the dancers to begin again. (1943, 6)

The Quadrille had numerous versions. In the 19th century, a complete Quadrille usually had five or six parts to different tunes separated by pauses. Each part consisted of an introduction; the first change, or the verse, where only certain couples did the main figure; the chorus for everyone; the second change, where the other couples repeated the verse; and a finish (Owens 1949, 37–38). In the United States, Americans dropped the initial eight measures, added a prompter, increased the tempo, and reduced five or six parts to three by combining figures.

The first Quadrilles were the Plain Quadrilles or French Quadrilles, created in France and introduced to London society at Almack's in 1815. The most popular combination of figures consisted of four Contradanse figures followed by a Cotillon figure: Le Pantelon, L'Été, La Poule, La Frenis, and Le Final. This dance and variations of it appeared in nearly every ballroom program until the mid-19th century. Dancers experienced variety by dancing the figures to different tunes and styles of music, notably classical music and light opera (Harris, Pittman, and Waller 1994, 133; Alan Winston, e-mail to author, May 24, 2010).

Within a few decades, the Plain Quadrilles were replaced by the Lancers Quadrilles (or simply Lancers or Lanciers), most likely of English origin (Rossoff 1977, 6). The Lancers had five parts to specific meters: Part I, 6/8; Part II, 2/4; Part III, 6/8; Part IV, 6/8; and Part V,

4/4. For most of the Lancers figures, opposite couples danced together. During the Grand Square, a popular figure for Part IV, for example, all dancers simultaneously walked the outline of a square, mirroring the pathway of their opposite across the set. Part V of the Lancers usually involved marching in single-file or double-file lines (Cohen 2004, 5:286–287; Harris, Pittman, and Waller 1994, 65, 133).

During the 19th century, dancing masters published numerous resources for other dancing masters, prompters, and dancers. Dance manuals characteristically included sections about the benefits of dancing, etiquette and manners, body positions (almost all manuals included the five foot positions of ballet), dance vocabulary, descriptions of figures, and tunes. One of the most widely distributed manuals was *Dick's Quadrille Call Book and Ball Room Prompter* (1878), part of a series of how-to books (Shaw 1949, 40–41). As the number of Quadrilles proliferated in the 19th century, dancing masters in North America began to prompt the dances as they were happening to remind people which figures came next (Cohen 2004, 5:287; Mayo 2003, ix).

By the mid-19th century, American ballroom programs commonly featured the Cotillon dance game, Galop, Mazurka, Polka, Quadrille, Redowa, Schottische, Varsovienne, Waltz, and several hybrid variations of these dance forms. The Prompters enabled dances to become more complex, because dancers no longer had to memorize the figures ahead of time. In the Circassian Circle, for instance, the caller combined Quadrille figures and other dance figures into a sequence. Then, the dancers repeated the sequence over and over while progressing as couples in a large circle formation (Richardson 1960, 103–104). The invention of a prompter also facilitated mixers, or dances with constant partner changing.

American Adoption of European Dances

Americans generally followed European ballroom trends until the late 19th century. Some European dances became so well known in the United States that they gained the reputation of American, even if they barely differed from their original version. The Virginia Reel, for instance, strongly resembled its ancestor, an English Country Dance titled Sir Roger de Coverley that was first published in 1685 (Harris, Pittman, and Waller 1994, 59, 69–70). Similarly, the New England longways dances Money Musk, Petronella (also Pat'nella, among other spellings), and Hull's Victory were close replicas of Scottish dances (Harris, Pittman, and Waller 2004, 185).

In 1788, dancing master John Griffith (sometimes Griffiths) published *A Collection of the Newest and Most Fashionable Country Dances and Cotillions*, the first known American dance manual (Page 1976, 22). The number of American dancing masters and American dance manuals grew over the next century as the demand for social dance lessons increased. During the political upheaval and terror that followed the French Revolution, a large number of French aristocrats relocated to North America and pursued careers as dancing masters as well. French dances thrived in the United States after the American Revolution (1775–1783), in part because the French had helped Americans fight the British.

Ralph Page, caller and expert in New England Square Dance (also called Contra Dance), observed that many American dance manuals published between 1795 and 1816 contained both English and Scottish names for figures. He remarked, "That was just after the Revolution War, and, no doubt in many districts of New England, the English were far from being loved" (Harris, Pittman, and Waller 1994, 185). After the American Revolution, Americans renamed some European dance figures and dance titles. For example, Setting in English Country Dance and Scottish Country Dance became the Balance in New England Square Dance (Harris, Pittman, and Waller 1994, 185).

Most dancing masters in North America worked in a large city or traveled between cities, giving workshops and private lessons. The strong presence of dancing masters in New England and along the mid-Atlantic coast helped these populated and wealthy areas maintain a strong connection to European social dance fashions. However, dancing masters rarely went to the less populated and unprofitable areas, such as southern Appalachia and the rugged West. Therefore, people in remote and rural areas generally did not receive the same technical dance training as city dwellers, and they did not learn the most recent versions of European ballroom dances.

As city dance forms gradually made their way to remote and rural areas, blending and changing over time and distance, unique American dance forms emerged. The major influences on New England Square Dance were English Country Dance, Contradanse, the Cotillon, Scottish Country Dance, and the Quadrille. In southern Appalachia, original American solo step dances and group dances evolved from African

Americans, poor Europeans, and possibly Native Americans. From 1730 to 1750, approximately 250,000 Europeans migrated to the Great Appalachian Valley. The Cherokee also occupied this region until the 1838 Trail of Tears forced them west. As European migration into the valley continued, many Scottish, Irish, and German immigrants moved into the backwoods, far away from towns and beyond reach of dancing masters (Duke 1984, 7–9).

In the 19th century, millions of European immigrants entered the United States and settled in cities along the East Coast. Myriad Americans left the overcrowded cities and went west. Many New Englanders moved to the Midwest, so the dances of the Midwest in the 19th century somewhat resembled those of New England. In the 1840s, thousands of Mormons seeking freedom to practice their religion migrated from the Midwest, New England, and Europe to Salt Lake City, Utah. After the Civil War, a large number of white Southerners relocated to the west, and thousands of African Americans moved north. Dance and music traveled with the migration waves, and new dance forms evolved as different cultural groups came into contact.

At the time of the Louisiana Purchase in 1803, Cajun Land, the swampy bayou region between New Orleans and Texas, already had a thriving dance culture with influences from African Americans, Native Americans, and Europeans. The Cajuns (the word derives from *Acadians*) were of French heritage and originally had settled in Acadia, present-day Nova Scotia, in the 17th century. When the English took over Acadia in the mid-18th century, the Cajuns were killed or expelled. Most survivors relocated to the New Orleans area, which was established by a French Canadian in 1718, and later ruled by the Spanish from 1762 to 1800. France regained control of New Orleans in 1800 during the Haitian war for independence. During this tumultuous period of slave uprisings, thousands of white planters relocated from Haiti to the New Orleans area with their slaves.

The Cajuns retained much of their French Canadian identity but also intermixed with local groups. They adapted Cotillons, Contradanses, Quadrilles, and other European ballroom dances to their own music, a combination of 17th-century French music as played in Nova Scotia and music from the British Isles, Germany, Spain, the United States, and West Africa. The accordion, violin, and triangle were popular instruments in Cajun music (Duke 1987, 5–6, 45).

Slave laws in Louisiana were unique because of the French influence. The Code Noir, issued at Versailles in 1724, explicitly forbade sexual relations between whites and slaves. To evade the Code Noir, slave owners in Louisiana who impregnated their female slaves often freed those slaves and their offspring. The number of *gens de couleur* (people of color, or mixed-race people) grew in the late 18th and early 19th centuries. Free women of color, in effort to attract white upper-class suitors and improve their circumstances, organized quadroon balls ("quadroon" means one-quarter black, but usually any women of color were allowed to attend). The quadroon balls imitated European balls and lasted from about 1790 until the Civil War (Emery 1988, 149–154).

In 1848, Mexico ceded its territories above its current border, granting the United States ownership of land to the Pacific Ocean. The California gold rush the following year triggered an influx of migration to the West Coast. By this time, California already had a strong dance culture connected to Native Americans and the Mexican rancho system. From about 1828 to 1846, the Mexican government had given large lots to government officials and settlers to raise livestock. The pastoral ranch lifestyle included frequent social gatherings with dance and music. Most of the rancho dances were popular French and Spanish ballroom dances, and they came to California by way of Mexico. Musical accompaniment for these dances included the flute, harp, mandolin, *vihuela* (guitar), violin, and vocals (Vandervoort 1999, 70, 72).

In the 19th century, remote and rural American community dances occurred in numerous settings, including town halls, dance halls, churches, firehouses, schoolhouses, private homes, barns, and the outdoors. In 1867, farmers established a cooperative called the National Grange of the Order of Patrons of Husbandry, or simply the Grange, and built grange halls that also hosted dances. These dances went by a variety of names, including junkets, barn dances, hoedowns, heel-burners, shindigs, fiestas, and fais do dos. The most common term for a dance event was simply a "dance" or "square dance." Square dances happened for a number of reasons, including weddings, holidays, corn shuckings, sheep shearings, quilting bees, barn raisings, roof raisings, or harvests, or simply because a fiddler was in town. In some rural communities, however, dances only happened around Christmas and the New Year, because farming families were preoccupied with work and church the rest of the year. People learned about dances through word of mouth, invitations, newspapers, or announcements posted in the town's general store (Tolman and Page 1937; John Wheeler, interview by author, August 20, 2009).

In some parts of the Midwest and South, 19th-century evangelical religious revivals forbade all dancing and condemned the fiddle as the devil's instrument. Still, many people continued to dance in the form of play-party games. For these games, dance figures and positions were modified to appear different than actual dancing. Also, the games did not have instrumental accompaniment, and instead were accompanied by hand clapping, foot stomping, and singing (Mayo 1943, 8). Play-party songs that have survived over several generations include "Skip to My Lou," "All Around the Mulberry Bush," and "London Bridge" (Rossoff 1977, 8).

European dances dominated North American ballrooms until the American Two-Step craze began around 1890. The Two-Step was a simple dance in 2/4 or 4/4 time that entailed marching chassés steps. The Two-Step flourished in part because of its suitability for "March King" John Philip Sousa's patriotic marches. In 1891, Sousa's "The Washington Post March" fit the Two-Step so perfectly that the dance sometimes was called the Washington Post or the Washington Post Two-Step (Giordano 2007, 1:262–264). Regional styles and hybrid versions of the Two-Step popped up across North America and Europe. One of the most popular Two-Step dances was the Circle Two-Step (also called the Paul Jones), a mixer where the dancers began in a large circle, broke away with a partner for the Two-Step, reformed the circle and found a new partner, broke away for the Two-Step, and so on (Shaw 1949, 398–399). The Two-Step declined during the Tango and animal-dance craze and was replaced by the One-Step and the Foxtrot in the 1910s (see chapter 2). The Two-Step was an important turning point in American social dance history because it proved that original Americans dances could compete with European dances in the ballroom and beyond.

American dances that evolved in remote and rural areas drew heavily from the popular European dances of the 18th and 19th centuries. Some communities preferred group dances and avoided couple dances altogether, whereas other communities incorporated group dances and couple dances into the same event. In the early 20th century, as part of a burgeoning urban folk dance movement, American rural dances of European origin were embraced as valuable American folk dances. Native American dances and African American dances generally were dismissed, and non-European influences on American Square Dance were not recognized until much later. At this time in the United States, according to the 1900 census, 88 percent of the U.S. population was white, and 86 percent of the foreign-born population came from Europe. Whites accounted for about 98 percent of the population in the Midwest and New England, 95 percent of the population in the West, and two-thirds of the population in the South.

4

Origins of the Folk
Dance Movement

Millions of Italians, eastern Europeans, and Jews migrated to American cities in the last quarter of the 19th century until World War I. By 1900, in large cities, including New York City and Chicago, the new immigrants and their children accounted for nearly two-thirds of residents (Tomko 1999, 2). The newcomers looked and behaved differently than the former residents. They wore different clothing, spoke different languages, and practiced different religions. They were perceived as a threat to the Anglo-Saxon Protestant identity that had come to define Americanness. Most of them were illiterate, unable to speak English, and unable to perform skilled labor. They also were viewed as a threat to job security.

In the late 19th century, educators and social reformers in the United States and England launched several social reform initiatives to alleviate urban anxieties and rejuvenate the national (Anglo) spirit. In both countries, the rise of industrialism had contributed to overpopulated cities, stifling living conditions, unsanitary and dangerous streets, and long workdays with pathologically repetitive movements performed on machines of questionable safety. The working class enjoyed few leisure outlets beyond music halls, which had the reputation of harboring immoral activities. As more and more people left rural areas for cities, a new urban lower class developed, comprised of people who were willing to work for lower wages than the previous lower class. Women and children commonly joined the workforce to abate economic hardship.

Physical Training for Health and Morals

From the mid-19th century through the early 20th century, a muscular Christianity movement that linked moral strength to physical strength occurred in England and the United States. The movement inspired such institutions as the Young Men's Christian Association (YMCA, or the Y). George Williams opened the first YMCA in London in 1844. At first, Ys served as dormitories that catered to the spiritual and mental development of young Christian men. Within a few decades, Ys began to incorporate physical training and sports programs. Military drills and gymnastics were popular types of physical training for young men at this time. By 1920, several hundred YMCAs, along with Ys for women, African Americans, and Jews, had been established in the United States and England.

For most of the 19th century, physical trainers in Europe and North America followed the German and Swedish gymnastics methods for men, pioneered by Friedrich Ludwig Jahn and Peter Henry Ling, respectively. After a failed revolution in 1848, German political refugees introduced the German method to the United States and England. The German method focused on muscular development. The Swedish method, on the other hand, focused on suppleness and was the most popular method by the 1870s. Around this time, Dudley A. Sargent also developed an American gymnastics method that incorporated weights, balls, and other objects. Sargent's method targeted specific muscle groups and was based on an individual's unique body shape and needs. By the 1880s, the Sargent gymnastics method was integrated into most Normal Schools, which trained schoolteachers to teach physical education (Walkowitz 2010, 28).

Some physical trainers incorporated rhythmic exercises known as gymnastics dancing into their gymnastics programs. In *Gymnastics Dancing* (1920), S. C. Staley and D. M. Lowery trace the origin of gymnastics dancing to ancient Greece. The authors suggest that gymnastics dance training continued in ancient Rome and Medieval Europe for military purposes. Gradually, though, physical training and dancing in general declined as Europe experienced a wave of asceticism that advocated depravity of the flesh. The European Renaissance cultivated renewed interest in physical training, and Girolamo Mercuriale's *De Arts Gymnastica* (1569) marked the beginning of the modern physical education movement. By the 18th century, physical trainers had readopted dance exercises into gymnastics programs. In 1793, Guts

Muths published *Gymnastics for Youth*, the first known publication to use the term "gymnastic dance" (Staley and Lowery 1920, 3–7).

In the 19th century, some physical trainers used singing and piano music to accompany their classes. As early as 1814, Francisco Amorós, a Spanish physical trainer who worked in Paris, emphasized singing to enhance the pleasure of exercise. Amorós's *Gymnastics and Morals* (1830) helped enhance the status of dance and music as part of physical training. Catherine Beecher girls' school in Cincinnati, Ohio, which opened in 1837, offered a physical training program that included graceful marching, skipping, and hopping rhythmic exercises to music. Dioclesian "Dio" Lewis, who pioneered a vigorous gymnastics method for men, discussed rhythmic exercises to music in his book *New Gymnastics* (1862). From 1865 to 1885, musical drills, artistically arranged exercises put to music, were popular in the United States and England and laid the groundwork for a gymnastics dancing movement (Stanley and Lowery 1920, 8, 11–13).

Staley and Lowery point to W. G. Anderson, head of the Brooklyn Normal School of Gymnastics, as the person who popularized gymnastics dancing in the United States. Anderson had studied Russian ballet and various step dances of Europe and southern Appalachia. Starting in 1887, Anderson taught gymnastics dancing at the Brooklyn Normal School of Gymnastics, Yale University, and at Chautauqua Assemblies (Staley and Lowery 1920, 14–15). Chautauqua Assemblies were educational centers that began in New York in 1874, as part of a nationwide adult education movement that escalated during the Progressive era (1890s–1920s).

In *Sex and Education: A Fair Chance for Girls* (1873), physician Edward H. Clarke suggested that intense exercise overstressed women's fragile physiology and weakened their reproductive organs. In the last quarter of the 19th century, physical trainers sought to develop an exercise system specifically for women. At the turn of the century, François Delsarte invented a set of gentle movement and breathing techniques that were deemed appropriate for women. Around the same time, Lois Fuller, Ruth St. Denis, and Isadora Duncan pioneered aesthetic dance (sometimes esthetic dance, classic dance, or Greek dance) as an alternative to music hall entertainment in the United States. Melvin Gilbert officially introduced aesthetic dance into physical training at the Harvard Summer School of Physical Education in 1894. Aesthetic dance was considered a valuable type of exercise for young women, particularly the social elite. As the number of girls and women at educational

institutions increased, gymnastics dancing and aesthetic dancing answered their perceived fitness needs (Walkowitz 2010, 28–30; Staley
and Lowery 1920, 16–17).

Arts and Crafts, Youth Clubs, and the Folk Revival

In the latter half of the 19th century, an Arts and Crafts movement also
tried to counteract the dehumanizing effects of overcrowded cities and
redundant machine work. John Ruskin, art and social critic, laid the
foundation for the Arts and Crafts movement by encouraging manu-
facturers to bring greater creativity and pleasure into labor. William
Morris, an influential socialist who believed in the redemptive power
of artisan labor, promoted the Arts and Crafts movement with his
decorative-arts firm and personal handiwork. The Arts and Crafts movement rapidly spread in England, Scandinavia, and the United States.

Several youth clubs also appeared at this time, focused on nature
and the physical and moral development of children. William Alex-
ander Smith founded the Boys' Brigade in Glasgow, Scotland in 1883.
Ernest Thompson Seton organized the Woodcraft Indians for boys
in 1902. The same year, Ohio educator A. B. Graham Daniel started
4-H, a club for boys and girls, inspired by a series of agricultural projects in the late 19th century directed the future of rural youth. In
1905, Daniel Carter Beard organized the Society of the Sons of Daniel
Boone, which in 1909 became the Boy Pioneers. In 1907, Sir Robert
Stephenson Smyth Baden-Powell, with encouragement from Smith,
left the Boys' Brigade and founded the Scouting movement in England. His sister, Agnes Baden-Powell, organized the Girl Guides in
1910. Back in the United States, Seton, Beard and other youth group
leaders were preparing for the Boy Scouts of America, which officially
began in 1910. Juliette Gordon Low founded the Girl Scouts of America
in 1912. Also in 1912, Luther Halsey Gulick Jr. and his wife, Charlotte,
incorporated the Camp Fire Girls of America.

The Arts and Crafts movement, heightened interest in rural life, and
recognition of the rejuvenating effects of nature all contributed to a folk
revival movement (Walkowitz 2010, 37). In the late 18th century, German philosopher Johann Gottfried von Herder had introduced the concept of *das Volk* ("the folk") a peasant class that embodied the true spirit
of a nation and whose lives were uncorrupted by homogenizing pan-
European influences (Cohen 2004, 3:29). In the 19th century, Europeans

coping with the challenges of urbanization, industrialization, and foreign occupation nostalgically embraced the concept of the pure and wholesome peasant. Anthropologists, folklorists, musicians, and other collectors traveled to rural areas to document traditions including poetry, rituals, games, and celebrations. Many collectors immersed themselves in folk songs, which, in contrast to the licentious music halls songs, were said to possess "unsophisticated, primitive, genuine, simple beauty of common emotion" (Walkowitz 2010, 33). Although collectors documented rural dances as part of folk traditions, the label "folk dance" did not exist until the 1890s (Cohen 2004, 3:29–30).

The Folklore Society was founded in 1878 in England. The American Folklore Society arrived a decade later in 1888. The earliest organizations dedicated to folk dance were founded in 1893 in Sweden, *Svenska Folkdansens Vänner* or Friends of Swedish Dance, and in 1901 in Denmark, *Foreningen til Folkedansens Fremme* or Danish Association for the Promotion of Folk-Dancing. The number of folklore, folk song, and folk dance organizations and societies grew over the next two decades. These groups produced handbooks, journals, photographs, recordings, recipes, costumes, props, and other cultural artifacts. They organized workshops, demonstrations, theatrical exhibitions, festivals, open houses, and other social events. Early folk dance teachers frequently consulted these groups when they needed materials (Cohen 2004, 3:33).

Settlement Houses, International Institutes, and Folk Schools

The 19th century Arts and Crafts, back-to-nature, and folk revival movements collectively informed the curriculum at settlement houses, international institutes, and folk schools. Social reformers believed that these centers would help the poor and disenfranchised improve their circumstances, which, in turn, would help society progress. Dance historian Mirjana Laušević elaborates, "This progress was not to be achieved through further industrialization and alienation, but through democracy, cultural pluralism, equality, [and] mutual appreciation" (2007, 73). In the United States, settlements and international institutes catered to the new wave of immigrants from southern, central, and eastern Europe. These centers were run by middle class and upper class volunteers, usually of Anglo-Saxon Protestant heritage, who aspired to help the immigrants assimilate into the American (Anglo) way of life. Many of the volunteers were daughters and wives in affluent families.

In 1884, Samuel Augustus Bennett founded Toynbee Hall in London, a Christian-inspired settlement house named after the social reformer Arnold Toynbee. Stanton Coit, leader of the Society for Ethical Culture, visited Toynbee Hall in 1886. A year later, in 1887, Coit established the first American settlement house, the Neighborhood Guild, in the Lower East Side of New York City. Jane Addams and Ellen Gates Starr visited Toynbee Hall in 1888, and within a year they opened the Hull House in Chicago. In 1893, Lillian Wald established the Henry Street Settlement in New York City. The United States boasted over 100 settlements by 1900 and over 400 settlements by 1910, many of them built near recent immigrant communities (Walkowitz 2010, 35; Lauševic 2007, 73).

Mary Wood Hinman is the earliest known American teacher of folk dances. As a young adult, in the 1890s, she gave folk dance lessons in her Chicago living room to alleviate her family's economic hardship. In 1909, Hinman explained some of the outcomes she witnessed in her 12 years of teaching ballroom dancing and folk dancing at Chicago's Hull House,

> [F]irst, the men gained the American attitude of respect for women, which they knew nothing of in their life in the other country; and second, they learned the value of self-respect. By letting the young people come for one evening a week in a clean, well-aired hall, with good music, good floor, and rules of politeness and formality maintained, they lose their desire to go elsewhere for this necessary social intercourse. They here gain healthy exercise, social intercourse in a pleasant setting and enough social technique to make them self-respecting. There seem to be no better, quicker, or surer way of obtaining our first hold on the young people we want most to bring off the street. These young men and women who crave social life seem to have no proper way open to them. (Gulick 1910, 75–76)

Hinman added that dance classes gave the immigrants "reliability," and they received better positions from their employers as a result. Furthermore, second-generation immigrant children learned to appreciate their heritage and to have better relationships with their parents after learning the songs and dances of their parents' homelands (Gulick

1910, 77). In 1904, Hinman opened the Hinman School of Gymnastics and Folk Dancing in Chicago and the Hinman Normal School to prepare young women to teach dance in schools and settlement houses.

The international institute was another important site where volunteers taught immigrants folk dancing as a way to assimilate. In 1911, the Young Women's Christian Association (YWCA) developed the first international institute to help young immigrant women. By 1945, many of the institutes had broken away from their parent organization and become independent agencies that catered to both sexes. Alice Sickels, first executive director of the International Institute of Minnesota, explains how the folk arts helped immigrants overcome hurdles of assimilation,

> Every person needs the experience of belonging—of the *we* feeling. The immigrants' first step in this direction is to belong to some group of their own people. . . . The next step is for the individual to function in a group of people outside his own nationality, to become, in other words, a part of a larger community. And it is at this point that American assimilation of the foreign-born, and even of their children, is most retarded. . . . A collection of individuals becomes a group only on the basis of shared experience. . . . It was necessary to start where people were, and many of the immigrants were unlettered people from peasant villages. The sought-for common ground was the folk arts. People can enjoy watching a dance, listening to a song, looking at a beautiful tapestry, or eating delicious food together, even though they may have nothing else in common. (1945, 184–185)

International institutes, as well as settlements, regularly organized open houses, pageants, and festivals where the immigrants often took over the planning process. This kind of experiential learning was supposed to teach the immigrants about democracy (Sickels 1945, 184).

American social reformers extended the concept of the settlement house to southern Appalachia to address issues of poverty, education, and ethics through social services and recreation. Rural settlements, sometimes called mountain settlements, provided recreational clubs and taught cooperative farming and dairying. Some settlements promoted local song and dance traditions or play-parties. The Log Cabin Settlement of Asheville, North Carolina opened in1895. The Hindman Settlement School in Hindman, Kentucky was founded in 1902, after two years of social programming informally based out of tents. The Pine

Mountain Settlement, organized in 1913 in southern Kentucky, was an important site for the folk dance movement. It was here, in 1917, that song collector Cecil Sharp, from England, documented a southern Appalachian dance that sparked interest in adopting rural American dances into physical education and recreation programs (Walkowitz 2010, 35).

In addition to rural settlements, after 1896, U.S. Commissioner of Education Philander P. Claxton promoted the Danish folk school model in the South. Folk schools began in 1844 in Denmark, and *Folkehøjskole* actually translates as "people's high school." In 1925, in Brasstown, North Carolina, Olive Dame Campbell opened the John C. Campbell Folk School, named after her late husband, who traveled the mountains and document social conditions for the Russell Sage Foundation. During the trips, Olive Campbell documented American folk songs. The John C. Campbell Folk School held its first "short course" with a recreational dance and music emphasis in 1930. In 1938, Berea College in Kentucky founded a Christmas Country Dance School, designed to supplement the short course. The John C. Campbell Folk School, Berea College Christmas Country Dance School, and Pine Mountain Settlement School were important folk music and folk dance hubs, and they also supplied the recreational folk dance movement with teachers for decades to follow (Bealle 2005, 153–154).

Constructive Play and Folk Dance for Children

Progressive reformers believed that society at large would improve if children, the most impressionable members of society, learned to internalize values such as democracy, equality, responsibility, and loyalty. Educational theorist John Dewey suggested that these values were best learned through fun and organized play, not through books and lectures. Child psychologist Stanley Hall proposed that children's stages of development paralleled the neuromuscular history of the human race. In other words, he believed that children's mental capacity was comparable to that of lower races, such as the new immigrant groups for which settlement houses were designed. Hall's theory, by extension, implied that the new immigrants were childlike and unsophisticated (Laušević 2007, 74–75; Shay 2008, 78).

Luther H. Gulick Jr., director of physical training for New York City public schools, who is credited for introducing folk dancing to New York schoolchildren and sparking a nationwide public school folk dance movement, considered folk dancing as a type of organized play. He explained why play was critical to children's development,

> Play is for the whole child—for his heart, mind, and imagination, as well as for his arms, legs, and chest. Play is far more important than mere muscular activity. It is the most natural and the most potent expression of the child's personality. The future lies in it. (Gulick 1910, 17–18)

Dancing, Gulick suggested, was a preferred type of play for children, because "childhood is the time when the physical nature is most sensitive to rhythmical movement" (1910, 26). Gulick believed that dancing was especially suitable for girls, who generally did not engage in team sports and rigorous forms of exercise. Folk dancing was the most practical type of dancing for New York schoolchildren. It required little equipment, and large groups of children were able to exercise simultaneously in small spaces. Furthermore, folk dancing helped children internalize wholesome values, that would help them in everyday life (Gulick 1910, 36–17).

In 1903, Gulick founded the New York Public Schools Athletic League (PSAL) to promote team sports and physical exercise for city boys after school. Two years later, Jessie Bancroft organized the Girls' Branch of the PSAL, through which much of the early public school folk dance curricula was developed by Elizabeth Burchenal under Gulick's supervision. In 1906, Gulick and Henry S. Curtis, a former student of Hall, founded the Playground Association of America (PAA). Supervised playgrounds gave children a healthier alternative to playing in filthy streets and in stifling apartments. The urban playground movement began in the late 19th century in England and the United States, but it picked up significant momentum with the PAA (Walkowitz 2010, 27). In 1907, Gulick appointed Burchenal as the first chairperson of the PAA's Committee on Folk Dancing.

Burchenal's success with folk dancing through the Girls' Branch of the PSAL encouraged many New York City public schoolteachers to teach folk dancing in the classroom. In 1909, Burchenal became the inspector of athletics for the New York City Department of Education and officially introduced folk dancing into public school curriculum, triggering a nationwide school folk dance movement. May Day pageants with maypole dancing were among the most popular folk dance activities for schoolchildren, because they allowed students to perform what they had learned during the school year. Furthermore, Educators perceived the maypole dance as a democratic experience because it required equal participation from everyone (Walkowitz 2010, 60).

Burchenal's curriculum encompassed several nations, but Gulick's criteria informed her selection of dances. Gulick recommended folk dances in which "most of the individuals [were] active most of the time," that could be "done by the largest number in the most limited space," and involved "large arm movements of the trunk, arms, and limbs" (1910, 38–39). He also mentioned that the dances were to be "graceful," and not promote "habits of movement or posture that [were] are disadvantageous from the standpoint of health" (39). Finally, the dances were to be "sufficiently simple for children to learn," and their emotional content in "relation to the morals of our civilization" (40). Gulick advised avoiding dances such as the Virginia Reel, for which many dancers stood inactive, Javanese dances "with small movements of the wrist," and Native American dances "in which a considerable portion of the body is bent forward, the individual dancing with bent knees and in a crouching position" (38–40).

Maypole Dance for the Friendship Charity Fete, 1915. Courtesy of Library of Congress, Harris & Ewing Collection (LC-H261-5157).

In 1909, Burchenal published the first of her several teaching manuals, *Folk-Dances and Singing Games*, with descriptions of 26 dances and songs primarily from Sweden and Denmark. The same year, C. Ward Crampton, director of physical training for New York public schools, published *The Folk Dance Book*. A year earlier, in 1908, Caroline Crawford, an instructor at the Teachers College in Columbia University, New York City, had published *Folk Dance and Games*. Meanwhile, in Chicago, Mary Wood Hinman was developing ballroom and folk dance curricula for John Dewey's experimental schools, which later became the University of Chicago Elementary and High School. Hinman worked for Dewey from 1906 to 1919, and by 1923 she had produced five volumes of *Gymnastic and Folk Dancing* (*Solo Dances*, *Couple Dances*, *Ring Dances*, *Group Dances*, and *Tap Dances*, *Clogs and Jigs*, in order of publication). Burchenal and Hinman both traveled to Europe to collect dances and songs for their manuals.

Some schoolteachers used folk dancing as a form of organized play to complement physical training (later known as physical education), whereas others used folk dancing only for pageantry. School folk dance manuals covered a broad spectrum, from dances that researchers documented in European villages, to folkloric dances that professional choreographers composed. Some of the earliest folkloric dances for schoolchildren came from Louis H. Chalif, a Russian ballet dancer who founded the Normal School of Dance in New York in 1904. Chalif taught folk dancing at PAA events, university summer schools, and the Henry Street settlement, among other places. Chalif published his European folk dances into three volumes, organized by level of difficulty (Walkowitz 2010, 63; Lauševič 2007, 103).

Early folk dance manuals generally described dances, step by step, on one page, with the corresponding tune arranged for piano on the next page. Most manuals provided little to no information about how the dances originated, when they were done and by whom, who first documented them, and how they were adapted for schoolchildren. For classroom purposes, dance rituals that lasted hours or days had to be condensed into minutes. Non-English lyrics were translated into English. Foreign sounds and melodies were adapted for the piano and rearranged in the western classical style. In the classroom, children wore light-weight shirts and gym shorts or bloomers. For May Day and other special events, however, children generally wore white costumes made from inexpensive

52811

cheesecloth, and they danced to brass bands instead of the piano (Shay 2008, 79–80).

The English Folk Dance Revival

Initially, the majority of folk dances introduced to American public schoolchildren came from Sweden and Denmark. In the second decade of the 20th century, however, educators turned their attention to more English dances. On both sides of the Atlantic, social reformers sought to rejuvenate the Anglo or Anglo-American spirit they associated with their nation, a spirit that the romanticized English folk inherently embodied (Walkowitz 2010, 66). Factory managers perceived Anglo assimilation as a way to manage an increasingly multiethnic, multilingual workforce and improve production. During World War I, for example, Henry Ford founded the Ford English School in Detroit, which staged melting pot rituals in which workers in adorned in ethnic costumes entered a large pot, and then emerged on the other side in identical clothing, carrying little American flags (Haenni 2008, 233).

In England's settlement houses, which mainly provided services and education to poor nationals, volunteers encouraged young women and children to play and dance for their health and morale. In the 1890s, Dame Grace Kimmins created the Guild of Play curriculum while working at London's Bermondsey Settlement House. Educators on both sides of the Atlantic incorporated the Guild of Play material into school folk dance programs. Emmeline Pethick-Lawrence, musical director of the Espérance Club and Social Guild, a settlement house for young women that Pethick-Lawrence cofounded with Mary Neal in 1885, organized a performance of Scottish songs and dances at the club's Christmas party. In 1904, new musical director Herbert MacIlwaine presented Irish songs and dances at the party in 1903. Neal went to Cecil Sharp, a musician, music collector, and authority on English folklore who had just been elected to the committee of the Folk-Song Society (established 1898), to inquire about rural English dances (Walkowitz 2010, 70–72).

In 1899, during a Christmas vacation in Headington, Sharp had observed a group of quarrymen perform Morris Dance while William Kimber Jr. accompanied them on concertina. In 1905, Sharp told Neal about his encounter with the group and gave her Kimber's contact information. The Espérance girls learned some of the English dances, performed them at the Christmas party, and the audience was so thrilled that Neal and MacIlwaine decided to tour England with the group. Inspired by the girls' success, Sharp shifted his attention to dance. In 1907, Sharp and MacIlwaine coauthored *The Morris Book*, with a history of the dance form and descriptions of 11 dances to be taught in schools. The same year, Sharp officially introduced English songs and dances to public schools as part of the Education Act. Also, a small group of educators including Neal and Sharp met to discuss a permanent folk dance organization. The English Folk Dance Society (EFDS) later formed in 1911 with Sharp as the honorary director (Walkowitz 15, 71–78, 85).

In 1909, Sharp published *The Country Dance Book,* which described 18 traditional dances he had observed in West Country villages. The same year, researcher Nellie Chaplin uncovered Playford's volumes on English Country Dance at the British Library. Between 1912 and 1922, Sharp published five more volumes of *The Country Dance Book*, which included his interpretations of 158 Playford's dances. Neal published *The Espérance Morris Book* in two volumes, in 1910 and 1912 (Walkowitz 2010, 15, 74–77, 84).

As public interest in Morris Dance increased, Sharp and Neal debated about how the dances should be collected and performed. Sharp believed that trained experts should collect the dances, and that the dances should be performed with grace and technical precision. He even instituted a certificate program whereby he directed formal examinations to judge how well the dancers performed the dances he taught them. Neal, on the other hand, believed that the folk dances came from unlettered peasants, and that the folk dance movement belonged to the working class who danced for joy, not precision (Walkowitz 2010, 77–78, 87–88).

In 1909, the Chelsea College of Physical Education, where Sharp was instructing teachers, established a School of Morris Dance with Sharp as director. Sisters Maud and Helen Karpeles joined the school and formed the Folk-Dance Club, which held dance performances for which Sharp played piano. Also in 1909, Neal started a folk dance vacation school for teachers at her Littlehampton hostel, originally a retreat for Espérance girls to experience holidays. Soon after, the governors of Stratford-upon-Avon, birthplace of William Shakespeare, asked to host the school. In 1910, while Neal was out of the country, and against her wishes the governors gave the directorship of the vacation school to Sharp. George Baker, a Harvard professor, attended the school in 1911. In 1913, Baker returned to the school with Mary Wood Hinman and philanthropist Helen Osborne Storrow, who later would introduce English Country Dance to the Girl Scouts (Walkowitz 2010, 81–82, 84).

In late 1910, Neal and Florence Warren, lead dancer of the Espérance Girls' Club, sailed to the United States for a three-month Morris Dance teaching tour. When they arrived, though, they discovered that all of their engagements had been cancelled by one of Sharp's friends. Quite likely, the responsible party was Elizabeth Burchenal, who had been in contact with Sharp for at least two years and believed that Sharp, not Neal, best represented English dance. Nevertheless, Neal and Warren were able to reschedule their commitments. They conducted a successful Morris Dance tour in New York and Boston, reaching out to many schoolteachers, planting the seeds for the English folk revival in the United States. In the summers of 1913 and 1914, A. Claud Wright, a gymnast who was part of Sharp's exhibition team, also toured New England, teaching English Country Dance, Morris Dance, and Sword Dance (Walkowitz 2010, 92–95).

When England became engulfed in World War I, Wright cancelled his 1915 U.S. summer tour to join the Royal Air Force. By this time, Neal had left the folk dance movement to pursue work in women's suffrage. Sharp, who had traveled to Paris with his exhibition group in 1913 and 1914 to demonstrate Playford dances, was beginning to gain an international reputation. In 1914, theater director Granville Barker invited Sharp to arrange music and dance for his production of *A Midsummer Night's Dream*, and, in December of that year, Barker invited Sharp to repeat his work for the New York production of the play (Walkowitz 2010, 85, 87, 108).

After Sharp completed his work on *A Midsummer Night's Dream* in New York, he began to investigate other economic prospects with English dance in the U.S. He focused on the historical Playford dances and overlooked the contemporaneous reels, jigs, and hornpipes of England's countryside. His initial attempts at lecturing proved unprofitable, but then Burchenal arranged for Sharp to teach dance at Susan Gilman's renowned dance studio in New York. Sharp was well received, and Gilman transformed her studio into a hub for English Country Dance in New York. Soon after, Sharp embarked on a three-week teaching tour in Boston and Pittsfield, Massachusetts and

Pittsburgh, Pennsylvania. In March 1915, a group of English Country Dance enthusiasts met with Sharp to establish an American branch of the EFDS. At a second meeting, they decided the organization would be based in New York, with Baker as president and Storrow as secretary. In 1916, Storrow assumed the presidency, a role she held until her death in 1944 (Walkowitz 2010, 102, 110, 112–113, 135).

Throughout his career, Sharp, an ardent anti-suffragist, had many conflicts with women in leadership positions, aside from the wealthy philanthropists who supported his work, the women that he personally appointed to direct the American Branch, and his handpicked research assistant, Maud Karpeles. Burchenal was the only major folk dance leader involved with the founding of the American Branch who did not receive a leadership position from Sharp. Dance historian Daniel Walkowitz attributes this to a serious copyright conflict. Burchenal wanted to use some of Sharp's dances and songs in her publications, but Sharp felt that he would not benefit from the arrangement. At this time, many European folk dance manuals and handbooks were resold in the United States without the author's permission, as the United States did not acknowledge international copyright laws until 1988 (Walkowitz 2010, 144–146).

The rift between Sharp and Burchenal extended to the record industry. Burchenal had recorded English folk dance tunes prior to Sharp's arrival in December of 1914, and she sought to record more. When Sharp arrived, though, within a matter of weeks, he signed a contract with Victor Gramophone Company to make 20 records, each featuring one or two songs for English Country Dance (the Playford variety). A few months later, he oversaw the production of 10 more records by the Columbia Gramophone Company. By 1916, Sharp monopolized the English folk dance record production. By 1924, he had produced enough records to sustain an English folk dance movement with a standardized collection of tunes, each tune associated with a specific dance. In his writings, Sharp recommended that the English tunes be played at 124 beats per minute, but his recordings typically were 136 beats per minute. The fast tempi encouraged dancers to move on the balls of their feet with forward energy (Walkowitz 2010, 146–150).

In 1915, Wellesley College invited Sharp to organize a three-week summer school, so that the students could present English folk dances, songs, and games at their annual Tree Day/May Day pageant. The school met at a campsite in Eliot, Maine, and the students slept in tents. A violent rainstorm on the last week devastated the site, and the participants continued at a nearby conference center. Sharp brought Helen Kennedy (formerly Karpeles) and Lily Roberts, head of the Scarborough branch of the EFDS, to teach at the summer school. Roberts stayed in the United States, where she met her husband, Richard Conant, and directed the American Branch from Boston. Musician Charles Rabold participated in the 1915 summer school and became one of the first prominent teachers of English Country Dance in New York (Walkowitz 2010, 113, 134).

By the time Sharp set sail for England, after the 1915 summer school, he had established a loyal group of followers, concentrated in New York and Boston, who had the technical expertise, teaching proficiency, and financial means to carry forth his vision of an English Country Dance movement. By 1916, Sharp devotees had created additional EFDS branches in Chicago and Pittsburgh, and dancers were beginning to organize in Cincinnati, St. Louis, and Rochester. In 1916 and 1917, Sharp directed two more summer schools at the Massachusetts Agricultural School in Amherst. The 1917 school had low attendance, and the 1918 school was cancelled because of the war. In 1917 and 1918, Sharp also visited Helen Storrow's Pine Tree Camp, located on Long Pond in western Massachusetts, to teach English dances and songs to Girl Scouts and Girl Scout leaders (Walkowitz 2010, 132, 135, 141–142).

From 1914 to 1918, Sharp made several trips to the United States and almost singlehandedly shaped a transatlantic English folk dance movement that focused on Playford dances, paid some tribute to English Morris Dance and Sword Dance, and largely ignored the existing dances of England's countryside. He created a highly standardized activity with recorded tunes and certification programs to ensure that his ideas about proper dancing would be maintained. The Scottish Country Dance Society (later the Royal Scottish Country Dance Society), founded in 1923 by Jean Milligan and Ysobel Stewart, imitated the EFDS's emphasis on styling and certification. Some English and Scottish dances found their way into classrooms through the American branches of the English and Scottish dance societies. Because of Sharp's copyright and recording conflicts with Burchenal, however, and Burchenal's belief that all folk dance traditions were equally valuable, English folk dance never gained a dominant foothold in American public school folk dance curricula.

After Sharp's death in 1924, Douglas Kennedy, a former member of Sharp's Chelsea exhibition team, and husband of Helen Karpeles, took over directorship of the EFDS. When Conant's family responsibilities made her no longer able to direct the American Branch, Louise Chaplin became Boston's head teacher, and Kennedy appointed Marjorie Barnett, who had been trained by Sharp, as the national director in New York. Barnett left after one year to pursue a teaching position. In 1927, May Gadd, director of the EFDS Northumberland Branch, stepped into the role of national director of the American Branch. Gadd held the position for 45 years, until 1972, and made sure the American Branch and its successor, the Country Dance Society, which later separated from its English parent, remained true to Sharp's original vision. CDS became the Country Dance and Song Society in 1967 to be congruent with the English Folk Song and Dance Society, produced by the merger of the English Folk Song Society and English Folk Dance Society in 1932 (Walkowitz 2010, 125–129, 135).

The English dance summer camps in the U.S. continued after Sharp's death. The New York Centre ran a summer school in Becket, Massachusetts in 1924, and in East Otis, Massachusetts in 1925 and 1926. Also in 1925 and 1926, Storrow allowed the Boston Centre to run its summer school at her Long Pond campsite. A dance pavilion was built at the camp during those years, and it was named "C#" (# means "sharp" in western music notation), in honor of Cecil Sharp. The disparate activities of the New York and Boston branches were not good for a national movement, however, and Rabold successfully proposed to renew the summer school at Amherst in 1927. In 1933, Storrow offered the American Branch a permanent summer campsite at her Pine Tree Camp. In 1935, Storrow and Conant renamed the property Pinewoods Camp. When Storrow died in 1944, she willed the camp to the Conants, and Gadd directed the camp until her retirement in 1972. The organizations that used the camp unified as the Pinewoods Camp, Incorporated and purchased the property from the Conants in 1976 (Walkowitz 2010, 142–143).

5

American Folk Dance Activities

American anthropologists, musicologists, folklorists, and other interested people studied Native American and African American song and dance traditions in the 19th century. In the late 1870s, for instance, John Lomax, the son of an English immigrant, began collecting songs and dances from a former slave who worked at his family's farm in Texas. In the 20th century, Lomax and his sons, John Jr. and Alan, became prominent collectors of American folk music, exposing the public to many African American spirituals, cowboy songs, and "hillbilly" songs (Walkowitz 2010, 165). Even with such efforts, few Native American and African American traditions found their way into the folk dance movement.

In the first decade of the 20th century, American folk dance teachers predominantly taught northwestern European dances. At this time, many white Americans believed that the most valuable (white) American dance forms merely were watered down versions of more refined (civilized) European dances. Some Americans also believed that the United States was too new of a nation to have original folk dances. Cecil Sharp's fieldwork in southern Appalachia helped change this perspective and helped introduce American rural dances into the folk dance movement.

The Running Set

In 1915, Cecil Sharp was recovering from an illness at Helen Storrow's home in Lincoln, Massachusetts when he heard some of the folk songs that Olive Dame Campbell had collected while accompanying her husband on research trips in southern Appalachia. Sharp thought that the songs resembled old English ballads, so he theorized that the songs actually were English songs, brought by early English settlers and preserved in mountainous isolation for centuries. Sharp asked Campbell for her permission to conduct fieldwork in southern Appalachia, and Storrow funded the endeavor. From 1916 to 1918, Sharp and his former student, Maud Karpeles, spent about 12 months collecting songs in 70 to 80 small towns and settlements mainly in North Carolina, Virginia, Kentucky, Tennessee, plus a few days in West Virginia (Walkowitz 2010, 37–38, 119–120).

In 1917, at the Pine Mountain Settlement in Kentucky, Sharp observed a dance that was unlike anything he had ever seen. The dancers stood in a circle, and one couple (the active couple) visited the other couples (inactive couples) in the set, one at a time. When the active couple returned to their original position, the entire set danced a group figure together. Then the second couple became active and danced with each inactive couple. The dance continued until all couples had assumed the active role. A caller, usually one of the dancers, prompted the figures and sometimes called verbal patter. Patter was not movement instruction; rather, it completed the musical phrasing of the call and gave the dancers time to complete their figure. Variations of this dance form existed throughout southern Appalachia and the Ozarks. Sometimes, every other couple initiated the figure simultaneously in a much larger circle set to reduce the amount of inactivity (Cohen 2004, 5:686).

The dance that Sharp observed at the Pine Mountain Settlement did not have a name. The participants referred to it simply as "dancing." Sharp named the dance the Running Set, published it in his *Country Dance* series, and proposed that it was a survival of an ancient English dance that predated Playford's time. His theory was based on the similarity of Running Set to old English children's games and the absence of courtly gestures (bows and curtseys). Problematically, Sharp's theory overlooked two centuries of backwoods cultural exchange among African Americans and European settlers of diverse

Sicilian Circle formation at a 2009 English Country Dance event with caller Peg Hesley and the Hands Four band, in Cottonwood, Arizona. Author's archives.

origins. Fortunately, though, Sharp's discovery of this dance inspired American folk dance teachers, musicians, and researchers to consider the value of studying American dance and song traditions (Cohen 2004, 5:286–287; Walkowitz 2010, 274).

The term "Running Set" became associated with a four-couple square formation, an unintentional consequence when Sharp proposed the four-couple square as most effective for educational settings, and Karpeles subsequently published additional figures for the Running Set that were actually New England Quadrille figures. By the late 1930s, folk dance teachers had institutionalized the Running Set in their curriculum as a four-couple dance form. The variation that involved every other couple dancing simultaneously in a larger circle became known as the Big Circle Dance or Big Set Dance and sometimes the Sicilian Circle. The formation was comprised of two-couple sets, with partners facing each other. At the end of each sequence, the partners passed by each other to face a new couple from another set (Cohen 2004, 5:287–288; Mayo 2003, 2).

Rural Dance Research and Radio Programs

Cecil Sharp's "discovery" of the Running Set was timely, in the midst of World War I (1914–1918). The outcome of World War I demonstrated to U.S. citizens their nation's superpower capability. Consequently, white Americans began to recognize that their own regional and national traditions were valuable, not simply watered-down versions of the European trends they had imitated since colonial days. Around this same time, Sharp drew nationwide attention to southern Appalachian dance. Although he endorsed the idea that the Running Set was an old English dance, some folk dance teachers challenged Sharp's mischaracterization through their own rural dance research.

In 1916, Elizabeth Burchenal resigned from the Public Schools Athletic League and became assistant state inspector of the Military Training Commission of the New York State Department of Education. The following year, she and Luther H. Gulick organized the American Folk Dance Society. In 1918, Burchenal published *American Country Dances: Twenty Eight Contra Dances, Largely from the New England States* under the auspices of the American Folk Dance Society. She explained her ideas about American folk dance in the preface:

> [I]t has often been said that our country has no folk-music or folk-dancing of its own other than that of the American Indian! We are to-day a nation of immigrants, not of Indians, and the folk-traditions that are most essentially our own are those which have developed (from traditions brought to us by our early immigrants) into something peculiarly our own. (v)

In *A Time to Dance: American Country Dancing from Hornpipes to Hot Hash*, about the history of dancing in rural America, author Richard Nevell describes Burchenal's book as "the first one of its kind to point out the simple virtues of the old dances, not as artifacts of history, but as a worthwhile physical activity" (1977, 62).

Around 1920 Grace Laura Ryan, a physical education teacher at Central Michigan Normal College (later Central Michigan University), began to document rural midwestern dances to supplement the European folk dances being taught to American schoolchildren. She compiled her research, along with some dances from the Rocky Mountains and southern Appalachia, in *Dances of Our Pioneers* (1926). The book focused on Quadrilles or Square Dances (Ryan used the terms interchangeably), but it also described longways dances, circle dances, and couple danced. Initially, A.S. Barnes & Company, a New York–based publishing company that produced many of the early folk dance manuals, rejected Ryan's book due to perceived lack of demand. When Henry and Clara Ford published *Good Morning,* a manual with descriptions and tunes for popular 19th century ballroom dances, A.S. Barnes reconsidered the potential market for books about traditional European American dance forms and decided to publish Ryan's book (Casey 1981, 31).

In the 1920s, the Texas Folklore Society, an American Folklore Society branch founded by John Lomax Sr. in 1909, published at least two articles about rural dance in the west, including J.R. Craddock's "The Cowboy Dance" (1923) and Roy S. Scott's "The Cowboy Dance of the Northwest" (1925). In 1925, Neva Boyd and Tressie Dunlavy wrote *Old Square Dances of America,* based on Dunlavy's fieldwork in southwestern Iowa. In 1927, Kathryn Blair published an article titled "Swing Your Partner," about rural dance in Kentucky, in the *Journal of American Folklore.* All of these publications foreshadow a nationwide infatuation with rural square dance as the most representative type of American folk dance. No doubt Henry Ford's old-fashioned dance revival, which reintroduced Quadrilles into ballrooms and schools, heightened scholars' and teachers' curiosity about similar rural dance forms.

The adoption of American rural dance forms into public schools and urban dance venues happened slowly through the 1930s. At first, polite society perceived rural dance forms as "not snappy enough" and "not sophisticated enough" (Marron and Marron 1944, 4). With the introduction of the radio into the average home in the 1920s, white middle-class Americans turned their attention to energetic jazz music played by brass bands. Furthermore, during prohibition (1920–1933), Cuba became a hotbed for wealthy American tourists, and many of these tourists developed a taste for music based on West African rhythms. Affordable automobiles manufactured by Henry Ford's plant in Michigan enabled more Americans to travel longer distances in less time to attend a dance. Ironically, Ford cars took many Americans to the "licentious" dance halls that featured jazz music and dance, which Ford so fervidly opposed.

Arthur Murray launched the radio-dance concept in 1920, when live music at the Georgia Tech campus was broadcast to dancers on a roof in downtown Atlanta. In 1924, George D. Hay organized the first *National Barn Dance* radio broadcast on WLS in Chicago with old-time fiddling live in the studio. The following year, Hay moved to

Tennessee and started a program on WSM called *Barn Dance*, which in 1928 became *The Grand Ole Opry*. Barndance radio programs flourished across North America in the 1920s and 1930s, popularizing hillbilly jamborees with southern Appalachian musicians as well as New England Singing Quadrilles, for which callers matched their voice to the melody (Cohen 2004, 5:686). In *The Folk Dancer*, folk dance leader Michael Herman stated that most of these programs played music suitable for listening, but not for dancing (Herman 1944 3:6, 14).

Dancing through the Depression

Adult recreation grew significantly in the first three decades of the 20th century. In *Studies in the Social Aspects of the Depression* (1972), originally published in 1937, Jesse Steiner explained that during the 1920s, numerous recreational activities were sponsored by government agencies, philanthropists, churches, and businessmen as part of social reform initiatives to counter the "demoralizing influence of unwholesome and degrading amusements" (1). The nature of recreation changed, however, when the depression hit in 1929 and organizations and donors curtailed their budgets. People looked for less expensive activities to fill a growing amount of leisure time, a result of unemployment and decreased work hours. Membership increased at public golf courses, tennis courts, bathing beaches, swimming pools, and hobbyist clubs (Steiner 1972, 38).

For affluent intellectuals, musicians, and artists, English Country Dance was more affordable than ski trips and country club memberships. In 1924, the English Folk Dance Society's Boston Centre had about 200 members and the New York Centre had 382 members. By 1931, the New York membership had grown to 655 people in 15 dance groups, many of them located in prestigious suburbs. By 1934, San Francisco and Palo Alto, California, had their own branch centers. A total of 17 branch centers existed by 1938, and each branch organized local dance events and relayed information about regional and national events, such as the Pinewoods Camp. All branches communicated with the parent organization in London as well as the American Branch headquarters in New York (Walkowitz 2010, 133).

English Country Dance was not accessible to everyone, however. In rural communities, people often struggled to make a living. They had little time for leisure and had few organized recreational activities.

In the late 1920s, Lynn and Katherine Rohrbough, graduate students at Boston University's School of Theology, recognized a need for fun and wholesome activities for church groups. With a group of students, the Rohrboughs created a game book and recreation kit for church parties. The kit met with high acclaim, so the married couple went into the publishing business as the Church Recreation Service. In 1929, they moved to a farm near Delaware, Ohio, and made their barn into a publishing firm.

In the early 1930s, the Rohrboughs traveled the United States as church recreation leaders, teaching and collecting songs, dances, and games. During their travels, they encountered Chester and Margaret Graham, who directed the Ashland Folk School in Michigan from 1928 to 1938. The Grahams introduced the Rohrboughs to recreational folk dancing (Houston 2006, 3). When the Rohrboughs returned to their farm, they took the name "Cooperative Recreation Service" and published several pocket-size books, including *Play Party Games* (1930 and 1932), *Quadrilles* (1931), *Singing-games* (1938), *Square Dances of the Great Smoky Mountains* (1939), *American Folk Dances* (1939), and *Favorite Square Dances* (1941). These books served countless church groups, youth groups, recreational folk dance teachers, and other folk song and dance enthusiasts. The Rohrbough family sold the Cooperative Recreation Service to a group of friends in 1967, and the company continues as World Around Songs (World Around Songs, n.d.).

The Depression did not damper folk dance activities in New York City, where many second-generation immigrants had organized nationality groups to celebrate their cultural heritage. *The Folk Dancer* magazine, published by Michael Herman from 1941 to 1947, indicated that the most active nationality groups in New York City represented Denmark, Estonia, Finland, France, Hungary, Italy, Lithuania, Norway, Poland, Scotland, Sweden, Switzerland, Ukraine, and Yugoslavia. Some of these groups had been active since the early 1900s. Many nationality group events were off-limits to outsiders. Some group members did not want uninformed people to borrow and change their traditions, whereas others feared criticism and ridicule (Sickels 1945, 76). However, public exhibitions by nationality groups gave schoolteachers more material for their curricula and manuals.

In 1931, Elba Gursay, an Italian folk dancer in New York City, proposed a Folk Festival Council (FFC). Beginning in 1932, and lasting about a decade, the FFC, in collaboration with the Foreign Language Information Council, offered an annual workshop series called "Folk Dances and Songs of Many Peoples," directed at schoolteachers. The FFC hired many nationality groups and individuals who were neither trained dancers nor professional teachers. The workshops usually featured local Europeans and their American-born children, but the organizers also hired Native Americans, Indians, Japanese people, and other people who otherwise had minimal representation in the folk dance movement. William Graubard's American Folk Dance Group and Margot Mayo's American Square Dance Group also participated in the series (*Folk-News*, 8:1, 16). The workshops happened during the school year at the New School of Social Research, a progressive school that was founded in 1919 by several Columbia College faculty members who publicly opposed the war and had been censured by the college president. Educational theorist John Dewey was one of the first faculty members to teach at the New School (New School for Social Research, n.d.).

In the late 1920s and 1930s, public fairs and festivals filled the need for inexpensive group entertainment and introduced many people to folk dance. In 1927, Bascom Lamar Lunsford organized the first Mountain Dance and Folk Festival in Asheville, North Carolina, with prize money awarded to the best dancers and musicians. The dance exhibitions were organized by Sam Love Queen, a descendent of Irish immigrants and renowned step dancer in southern Appalachia. The 1938 festival featured the first known team step dance competition, and Queen's team, the Soco Gap Dancers, won the competition. Their routine consisted of freestyle step dancing while executing Big Circle figures, led by a caller. In 1939, the team was invited to perform their routine in Washington, D.C. for President Roosevelt, King George VI, and Queen Elizabeth of England. The Queen reportedly said that the Soco Gap Dancers' routine looked like the Clogging in her own country, and the label "Clogging" stuck for Appalachian step dancing (Duke 1984, 21, 31).

A wave of folk festivals swept the nation in the 1930s, organized by a growing number of dedicated folk dance enthusiasts. In 1932, Alice Sickels, executive director of the International Institute of Minnesota, organized the Folk Festival in St. Paul. The festival advisory council, all women, represented 18 different nationalities. One advisor, Florence G. Cassidy, had helped organize the Folk Festival Council in New York City. Sickels advertised the festival in local newspapers, stating that any nationality group could participate. The YWCA hosted the free three-day festival, and a wide range of nationalities participated. There were performances, costumes, cultural artifacts, stories, and an international array of refreshments available for purchase. The festival grew each year, expanding into an imaginary International Village based on Old World traditions, and it was renamed the Festival of Nations in 1939 (Sickels 1945, 75, 82, 105).

In 1933, Sarah Gertrude Knott, director of the Drama League of St. Louis, created the National Folk Festival Association (later incorporated as the National Council for the Traditional Arts). The following year, Knott organized the first three-day National Folk Festival in St. Louis. Unlike most other festivals that focused on audience spectatorship, Knott's festival included participatory workshops. For decades to follow, the festival represented a wide array of cultural groups and professions through instrumental music, songs, dances, and games (Casey 1981, 29). In 1938, Eleanor Roosevelt helped bring the festival to Washington, D.C., where it stayed through 1941 in order to lay the foundation for local folk festivals (National Council for the Traditional Arts, n.d.).

President Franklin D. Roosevelt's New Deal initiatives (1933–1936) helped further folk dance activities during and after the Depression. To begin, the Civilian Conservation Corps (CCC) built hundreds of roads, parks, campsites, and recreational facilities. The Mendocino Woodlands Camp in northern California, which went on to host folk music and folk dance camps throughout the summer, began as a CCC project in the 1930s. Secondly, the Works Progress Administration (the WPA was renamed the Work Projects Administration in 1939) employed several folk dance leaders. The WPA hired musician Michael Herman to attend FFC workshops and transcribe the nationality groups' music. Vytautas "Vyts" Beliajus edited *Lore* (1936–1939), one of the first folk dance magazines, with WPA funding. Fenton "Jonesey" Jones worked for the WPA as a caller and musician at a California senior center in the late 1930s. Jones helped pioneer a recreational Square Dance movement and recorded numerous singing squares for the McGregor record label, one of the first square dance record companies (Bob Dalsemer, e-mail to author, August 30, 2010).

The WPA Federal Writers' Project (1935–1939), directed by Henry Alsberg, also enriched the folk dance movement with new material. For the Folklore Project (1936–1940), for example, John Lomax Sr., Benjamin Botkin, and Morton Royce collected life stories, songs, sustenance practices, celebrations, and other types of cultural expressions related to different occupations and lifestyles, in order to create a comprehensive account of the groups of people in the United States (American Life Histories, n.d.). Just three years earlier, in 1933, Lomax and his sons, John Jr. and Alan, had pioneered the use of electronic recording machines to collect songs and stories in the field. Their research was funded by the American Council of Learned Societies and the Library of Congress's Folk-Song Archive (founded in 1928 as the Archive of American Folk Song, and now the Archive of Folk Culture hosted by the American Folklife Center) (Walkowitz 2010, 165; American Folklife Center, n.d.).

From 1936 to 1938, the Federal Writers' Project also collected life stories of 2,300 former slaves spread across the South (Born in Slavery, n.d.). Because slaves usually were illiterate, and slave owners took little care to document their slaves' music and dance traditions, these narratives provided valuable source material. Some narratives showed how European and African American dance traditions were combined in the 19th century, challenging the early 20th century perception that rural American dance forms solely evolved from European (or English) dances (Emery 1988, 100). Although WPA research about former slaves brought to light another realm of American dance traditions, it did little to further the image of American Americans in folk dance settings.

In the 1930s, white middle-class Americans could go to the cinema for a reasonable price and watch movies with nonthreatening white tap dancers, including Fred Astaire, Ginger Rogers, Eleanor Powell, and Shirley Temple. One of the most famous African American tap dancers from this decade, Bill "Bojangles" Robinson, had a smooth, reserved, upright style that contrasted with the Jitterbug. Folk dance teachers quickly recognized that Tap Dance could supplement folk dance in physical education. Furthermore, they believed that the more aggressive and loud nature of Tap Dance would appeal to boys, who were less attracted to aesthetic dances and European folk dances.

The first widely popular step dance manuals for schoolteachers, Mary Wood Hinman's *Clogs and Jigs* (1918) and Helen Frost's *The Clog Dance Book* (1921), set the standard for subsequent manuals (Frost 1931, 1; Duggan 1936, ix). In Hinman's manual, dance steps were called

Second graders and third graders in blackface for a May Day festival at the Ashwood Plantations, in South Carolina, 1939. Courtesy of Library of Congress, Farm Security Administration—Office of War Information Photograph Collection (LC-DIG-fsa-8c10160).

1s, 2s, 3s, and so on, based on the number of tap sounds made. Steps also had names that described their action, such as Toe Tap, Fall, Flop, Slap, and Chug. Frost's manual borrowed Hinman's terminology, and it also associated some step dances with characters from blackface minstrelsy. Subsequent Clogging and Tap Dance manuals in the 1930s and 1940s maintained this representation of African Americans, and the manuals sometimes included photographs of dancers in blackface. In this era, schoolchildren were known to Clog or Tap Dance (the terms were used interchangeably) in blackface for school pageants.

The Square Dance Resurgence

In the 1930s, American schoolteachers' and urban trendsetters' fascination with rural dance forms was just beginning. Increased leisure time for the unemployed masses, affordable automobiles, improved roadways, new state parks and campsites, and youth hostels increasingly brought urban Americans into contact with rural Americans. Some rural communities still had weekly dances, which were usually held on Saturday night. In *The Country Dance Book* (1937), authors Beth Tolman and Ralph Page described how wintertime skiers from cities began to adopt the rural New England dances,

> At first, of course, the city folks didn't mix in. You couldn't blame them. Heaven knows, there's nothing more bewildering than a mess of high-stepping country dancers trying to follow a caller who's faster than a cat lapping up chain lightning! The visitors sat by, smiled, and occasionally were awed. Some bold ones tried the more simple figures but found that there was all the difference in the world between a Portland Fancy of today and what they thought they knew as a Portland Fancy in the days of their dancing school youth. And as for foxtrots, no amount of skill in those would help in a country dance. And the "natives" didn't come to the rescue . . . not at first, that is. A combination of shyness and skepticism kept them back. But as soon as they realized that most city folks really wanted to learn the dances in a "serious "way, and that these people were not much different, after all, from themselves, then they opened up like umbrellas and were very generous in giving instruction. (1937, 21–22).

Tolman and Page's account of the skiers who embraced New England country dance became a popular anecdote for the beginning of a recreational Square Dance movement.

Slowly, American Square Dance began to appear in settings that formerly featured European folk dance. In the 1930s, the Swing & Turn Club at the University of Texas in Austin introduced Roy and Zibby McCutchan to West Texas Square Dance, and the couple later founded the Lone Star Club recreational group and the Lazy Eight Club exhibition group (Ron Houston, e-mail to author, November 16, 2010). In 1934, Ed Larkin founded the Old Time Contra Dancers, an exhibition group for New England Square Dance. At the New York City World's Fair in 1940, Larkin's group competed against Henry Ford's dance group and won (Nevell 1977, 93–95). Square Dance exhibitions at fairs and festivals, especially in cities, showed myriad city dwellers that rural dance forms could be smooth and elegant like refined ballroom dances, not rough and rowdy, as rural dances were stereotyped.

Swing & Turn Club at the University of Texas Women's Gym, 1939–1940. Courtesy of Society of Folk Dance Historians.

The Lazy Eight Club, 1951–1952. Courtesy of Society of Folk Dance Historians.

Dance historians generally trace renewed interest in rural Square Dance to Lloyd Shaw, a folk dance enthusiast and high school principal in Colorado Springs, Colorado. In the early 1930s, Shaw introduced European folk dances, New England dances, and play-party games to his exhibition group at the Cheyenne Mountain High School. As time passed, Shaw discovered that locating information about New England dances was not difficult, because these dances had been documented by dancing masters (Shaw 1939, 26). Similarly, play-party games and dances from southern Appalachia had been documented by Cecil Sharp and others. The dances of the western cowboys and pioneers however, were not well documented. Shaw attempted to fill this gap with *Cowboy Dances* (1939) and *The Round Dance Book* (1948).

For *Cowboy Dances* (1939), Shaw collected dance calls and descriptions by attending rural community dances and interviewing elderly callers. At rural dance events, Shaw noticed that the dancers responded to the callers' intonations more so than specific words. The participants knew the calls ahead of time, because the dances always were done the same way. Each community had its own dance collection or repertoire, and this repertoire gradually changed over time and sometimes this repertoire sometimes overlapped with that of nearby communities. Shaw demonstrated refined versions of the rural dances with his exhibition team, and he taught the dances to schoolteachers and recreational groups. He also organized callers' workshops that brought together leading callers from across the United States. This was the first step in creating a nationwide recreational Square Dance movement.

Folk Dance as Art

Folk dance exhibition groups typically modified dances for the stage, which some recreational folk dance enthusiasts tolerated and other abhorred. Frequently, exhibition groups that used elaborate costumes, balletic footwork, quick stepping, aerial lifts, interweaving formations, and intricate patterns convinced audience members to take up folk dancing as a recreational activity. Folk dance leaders increasingly recognized that recreational folk dance could benefit from theatricalized performances; and conversely, folk dance could inspire art. In 1918, Elizabeth Burchenal foreshadowed the merger of American folk dance with more "legitimate" forms of art,

[E]very effort should be made to encourage, preserve and assimilate this dancing and music, so that we may not only have these added resources for social enjoyment and recreation, but that our national life may be enriched with beauty and color and joy of living which may become the foundation of a yet undreamed-of development of art in this country. (1918, v)

In the early 20th century, Louis Chalif used European folk dance as inspiration for his composed dances, which were rooted in classical ballet. However, American modern dancers who used folk motifs in their choreographymade a much stronger impression.

In 1936, several professional dancers in New York City organized the First National Dance Congress and Festival at the 92nd Street Y (founded as 92nd Street Young Men's Hebrew Association in 1874). In the 1930s, modern dancers, including Martha Graham, Doris Humphrey (a student of Mary Wood Hinman), Charles Weidman, and Hanya Holm, were struggling for institutional support and recognition. William Kolodney, educational director for the 92nd Street Y from 1934 to 1969, allowed them to use the Y's Dance Centre. He envisioned the 92nd Street Y as a place where Jews especially could experience solidarity and gain upward mobility through the arts, even though the Y welcomed everyone. The Dance Congress consisted of modern dancers, ballet dancers, folk dancers, and Broadway-style revue dancers. Their goal was to initiate a movement to unite all dancers nationwide. The first event was eight days of panels, lectures, and performances. Several folk dance groups performed, representing the United States, Poland, England, Ukraine, Bohemia, and Sweden (Jackson 2000, 5–7, 70).

In New York City, modern dancers interacted with folk dancers and sometimes borrowed folk dance themes and movements. When modern dance became recognized as a legitimate art form, the success of modern dance compositions that used folk dance, no doubt, helped fuel the folk dance movement. For example, Agnes de Mille's *Rodeo* (1942), choreographed shortly before the Broadway hit *Oklahoma!* (1943), included a ranch house party and a hoedown, taking inspiration from American Square Dance. De Mille's fascination with folk dance continued throughout her career. In the 1950s, she created the Agnes de Mille Folk Dance Project, in which highly trained modern dancers turned folk dance into performance art.

As part of Cold War politics, the dance panel of the National Cultural Committee (NCC), part of the CIA-funded Congress for Cultural Freedom, selected the Agnes de Mille Folk Dance Project to represent the United States abroad. This was in response to the USSR and Soviet Bloc nations that sent professional folk dance groups, trained in ballet, around the world to spread Soviet propaganda. Funding for the Agnes de Mille Folk Dance Project never materialized. In 1962, though, shortly after the Cuban Missile Crisis, the NCC sent the more affordable Berea College Folk Dance Group to Mexico, El Salvador, Guatemala, Honduras, Nicaragua, Costa Rica, Panama, Colombia, and Ecuador (Walkowitz 2010, 196–197).

6

International Folk Dance

Recreational International Folk Dance clubs, representing dances from many lands, began in the Untied States in the 1930s and picked up momentum in the 1940s. At this time, American children (especially girls) experienced folk dancing in schools and youth groups, adults enjoyed folk festivals, and polite society advocated folk dancing as a wholesome alternative to dance halls. In comparison to the 1890s, the dominant group of white Americans felt less threatened by new immigrants, particularly because the Johnson-Reed Act of 1924 strongly favored immigration from northwestern Europe. Furthermore, Franz Boas' theory of cultural relativism, which suggested that all cultural groups were unique, was beginning to replace previous notions about a race-based ladder of evolution. When World War II (1939–1945) shed light on the importance of cross-cultural education and understanding, international folk festivals and RIFD clubs offered a practical solution to this social need.

Long before the printing press facilitated mass production of newspapers and books, festivals served to bring large groups of people together for education and celebration. The World's Fair (sometimes called the World Fair, Universal Exposition, or World Expo) began in 1855 as the Great Exhibition of the Works of Industry of All Nations, held at the Crystal Palace in Hyde Park, London. World's Fairs focused on science and technology through 1938. They showcased innovation, such as the telephone and Ford's automobile, and they marked important historical events, such as the opening of the

Panama Canal. Situated in the colonial era, naturally, these fairs also featured exhibits, performances, and foods from many lands. They were immersive experiences with colors, sounds, tastes, and smells.

Sabine Haenni's *The Immigrant Scene: Ethnic Amusements in New York, 1880–1920* (2008) shows that much cross-cultural, cross-gender, and cross-class interaction happened in the public life of large cities during the Progressive Era (1890s–1920s). Streetcars, elevated trains, subways, and automobiles increased mobility and gradually replaced horse-drawn carriages. Electric lighting improved safety for unaccompanied women, and mixed-sex leisure activities such as tennis became more common. Rooftop gardens and parks allowed diverse people to congregate and temporarily escape fast-paced city life. German American theaters, which were popular in large cities through World War I, provided an educational (legitimate) type of entertainment, in comparison to minstrelsy vaudeville (Haenni 2008, 70–71).

The German American theater, known as *Volkstheater* or folktheater, created a new type of public leisure space by melding diverse Americans into a community of consumers. The theater sold American goods such as candy and soda. Its playbills contained advertisements for German American businesses, encouraging audience members to visit these places for additional cultural experiences. Importantly, the German American theater demonstrated that German Americans were modern, and that the American public could find something valuable in their displays of collective identity. In the 1890s, Jewish and Italian immigrants opened their own theaters, borrowing the German American model. By the 1900s, though, these groups had to compete with other forms of popular entertainment, such as the nickelodeon and cinema. Jewish and Italian plays found their way into less reputable settings, such as music halls, saloons, cabarets, and cafés that sold alcohol (Haenni 2008, 57–59, 101–102).

In the 1870s and 1880s, white male bohemians (artists and intellectuals) ventured into eastern European neighborhoods and popularized "slumming" as an alternative leisure activity. In 1890, Jacob Riis drew further attention to city slums in his widely read *How the Other Half Lives*, with prose and photographs about New York City's highly congested Lower East Side. Shortly thereafter, George du Maurier's *Trilby* (1894), set in bohemian Paris, sold more than 200,000 copies in the United States and fueled an urban bohemian movement. By the early 1900s, bohemian style tourism was a regular part of New York

City. Mass-circulation magazines featured essays on slums' restaurants, stores, and inhabitants. "Rubberneck" automobiles tours took respectable whites on guided tours through Chinatown (a leisure space staged for Americans) and new immigrant neighborhoods (Haenni 2008, 42–43, 144–145).

In the 1910s, the cinema gave Americans the opportunity to escape everyday life without venturing far from home, and it offered a cheaper way to experience slumming. Myriad films were produced about Chinatown and immigrant neighborhoods, and these films helped white viewers negotiate the presence of "others" in their cities. Films such as *Traffic in Souls* (George Loane Tucker, 1913) and *Gretchen the Greenhorn* (Chester M. and Sidney Franklin, 1916) depicted northern and western Europeans as nonthreatening. Films about southern and eastern European usually featured corruption, counterfeiting, kidnapping, orphaned immigrants, mixed-up identities, and intergenerational conflicts. These types of films attempted to mobilize empathy and promote cross-cultural reconciliation (Haenni 2008, 146–147, 190–194).

Until the late teens, American entertainment venues encompassed a wide range of experiences. Vaudeville, drama, and cinema easily coexisted in the same space. Nickelodeons increasingly used live acts into their programs. Picture palaces borrowed the immersive sensory model of the World's Fairs. If a motion picture featured a particular immigrant group, palace employees often wore that group's national costumes and decorated interior spaces accordingly. Sometimes the staff sang national songs and served national foods. Program notes frequently advertised ethnic eateries where audiences could consume more of the culture. Many of these places were cabarets, which combined food, entertainment, and social dancing (Haenni 2008, 195–196, 204).

By the time RIFD clubs emerged, upper-class and middle-class white Americans regularly encountered immigrants (or impersonations of immigrants) as part of the public leisure culture. Furthermore, most white women and some white men knew immigrant songs and dances from their childhood physical education programs or afterschool activities. RIFD, therefore, was a natural extension of the folk dance movement into a more public realm. Elizabeth Burchenal anticipated this shift as early as 1922, when she wrote in *Folk Dances from Old Homelands*,

A definite movement has been underway to promote the popular use of folk-dancing as recreation for adults. . . . The demand for information and assistance in introducing it into general use, now coming from all parts of the country, indicates a quickening interest which may be the foreshadowing of a great popular use of folk-dancing as social recreation. (1922, x)

RIFD created a safe space for respectable white Americans to not only interact, but also to have physical contact with southern and eastern European immigrants and their children. Some African Americans and Asian Americans participated in RIFD, some even as club leaders, but they were vastly outnumbered by white Americans, including the grandchildren of southern and eastern Europeans who became recognized as white in the mid-20th century.

Early RIFD Clubs

The first known RIFD group evolved within a Unitarian organization called the Cosmopolitan Club (Cos Club) in Montclair, New Jersey. Elvira Fradkin and Pauline Hamilton founded the club in 1927 to promote international goodwill and understanding, following the demise of the League of Nations. The club met monthly from October to May, devoted its meetings to discussions about international affairs, and invited renowned speakers as well as students from New York City's International House. Each meeting had a theme and performance to a live band. The club members prepared costumes, songs, folk dances, and dramatizations of folk customs, festivals, and holidays. Membership quickly grew to 600, and there was a permanent waiting list. Club members formed their own educational and recreation groups within the Cos Club, such as language groups, a hiking group, and a recreational folk dance group (Houston 2004, 1).

Stella Marek Cushing, a folk dancer, writer, and musician, founded the Cos Club's RIFD group in 1931. Cushing died in 1938, and her student, Rose Grieco, then 23 years old, took over the group. Her sister, Barbara Grieco, became group leader in 1995. Barbara Grieco and Jeanette "Jay" Novak, a Cos Club member who notably introduced Doudlebska Polka to RIFD recalled that during World War II, Percival Brundage, a wealthy Cos Club member, hosted RIFD dances at his home for servicemen and female club members. Also, the club sponsored two benefit folk dance festivals at the Montclair High School to help Czech refugees. Some club members adopted English children who had been orphaned by the war, illustrating the community's strong humanitarian commitment. The RIFD branch of the Cos Club was not just about dancing; it was part of a much larger mission (Houston 2004, 2).

Folk dance historians usually trace the beginning of RIFD as a nationwide movement to the late 1930s, in three cities: Chicago, New York City, and San Francisco. By the time RIFD took hold, European and American folk dance activities were already happening in all of these places on a regular basis, in immigrant neighborhoods, settlement houses, international institutes, cultural centers, recreation centers, schools, and playgrounds. Vytautas "Vyts" Beliajus, a Lithuanian immigrant, is given credit for launching the RIFD movement in Chicago. Michael Herman and his wife, Mary Ann, are considered the leaders of the RIFD movement in New York City. Michael Herman was a second generation Ukrainian and professional musician. As a young man, he studied dance with Vasile Avramenko, teacher and choreographer of theatricalized Ukrainian folk dance. Mary Ann grew up in a mixed immigrant neighborhood in New York City, and she performed and taught Ukrainian dance prior to meeting Michael. In San Francisco, a Chinese immigrant named Song Chang encountered folk dances on a boat in Europe, and Chang's interest led him to Valborg "Mama" Gavander, who taught Swedish dance, songs, games, and crafts at her home in the Pacific Heights. In 1937, Chang invited three couples to join him and his wife for an evening of RIFD in their basement, and a club was born (Shay 2008, 83–86; Casey 1981, 22; Houston 2006, 3).

Beliajus taught dances that he had learned from his youth in Europe and dances he had picked up from the Lithuanian community in Chicago. In 1930, he founded the Lithuanian Youth Society and taught the group Lithuanian dances. They were invited to perform at the 1933 Chicago World's Fair. Audience members enjoyed the performance, and the group subsequently toured the Midwest and Canada. In 1936, the Chicago Park District hired Beliajus to teach folk dancing, and he learned more dances from the immigrant communities that lived around the parks. Beliajus traveled extensively to teach RIFD, and he taught a broad repertoire that included Jewish dances and Mexican dances. From 1943 through 1994, Beliajus also produced the folk dance magazine *Viltis* ("hope" in Lithuanian) an important source for

RIFD news, dances, music, costumes, customs, and recipes (Laušević 2007, 147–148; Shay 2008, 85–86).

An important catalyst for a nationwide RIFD movement was the 1939–1940 World's Fairs in New York City and San Francisco. Until this point, the World's Fairs had focused on science and industry. The 1939–1940 fairs represented a turning point in World Fair history, because they stressed cultural exchange and humanitarianism. For the New York fair, Building the World of Tomorrow, Patricia Parmelee of the Folk Festival Council organized the dance program. It included nationality group performances both years, as well as participatory folk dance evenings with Michael Herman the second year. In the first issue of the *The Folk Dancer*, from March 1941, Herman estimated that over 5,000 people joined in the folk dance evenings. He wrote,

> The success of the project was due to the fact that it was based on the realization that folk dances, one of the most colorful contributions by immigrants to this American culture, are NOT to be watched as just colorful entertainment, but should be PARTICIPATED in. (1:1, 1)

In 1940, Herman offered a RIFD series titled "Community Evening of Folk Dances of Many Lands" hosted at his Community Folk Dance Center, located at the Ukrainian National Home. The Community Folk Dance Center moved to the Polish National Home and the German National Home before its permanent location at 16th Street and 6th Avenue in 1951, when it was renamed the Folk Dance House. A typical dance session at the center lasted about three hours split between instruction of new dances and general dancing, when dancers made requests (Casey 1981, 22–23).

Herman described his folk dance followers as "free lance people" who took every opportunity to learn and do the dances of nationality groups. He wrote, "They are exponents of the true spirit and meaning of the folk dance because they dance not for nationalistic reasons, not for exhibition, but for the sheer joy of doing the dance" (1941, 1:5, 1). At the dance center, Herman usually taught the dances and played violin, and his wife often played piano. For special events, Herman sometimes hired nationality groups to play music and lead workshops. Herman often complained about the lack of good recordings for RIFD, so, with the help of David Rosenberg, he started the Folk

Dancer record label in 1948 (Houston 2006, 6). The Folk Dancer record label released over 300 records specifically for RIFD dancers (Shay 2008, 84).

The World's Fair in San Francisco, the Golden Gate International Exposition, featured nationality group performances and Chang's Folk Dancers (also Chang's and later Changs), an exhibition group that consisted of Americans from different ethnic backgrounds who did dances from different nations. There was no participatory folk dancing at the San Francisco fair, but hundreds of dancers joined Chang's group afterwards and similar RIFD clubs emerged in the Bay area. The California RIFD clubs were known for being more exhibition oriented than the East Coast groups, in part because the beautiful weather, popularity of cars, and availability of cheap spaces to rent facilitated folk festivals.

Chang resigned as director within a few years, but the group affectionately retained the founder's name when Virgil Morton took over. Madelynne Greene replaced Morton when he shipped off for World War II. Greene was one of several Chang dancers who made incredible contributions to RIFD. She organized California RIFD teachers' institutes, through which many new dances were introduced to RIFD, and she also founded Mendocino Folklore Camp in 1962. Other notable Chang dancers included Larry and Joanne Keithley, who started an RIFD group in Tokyo, Japan shortly after World War II. They built upon the foundation laid by Warren Nibro, a U.S. Army recreation specialist who had learned folk dances from Michael Herman before being stationed in Japan during the war. Keithleys' RIFD group boosted the image of American RIFD in Japan, especially when Prince Mikasa (youngest brother to the god-king Emperor Hirohito) and his wife, Princess Mikasa (Yuriko) Takagi, held hands and danced with regular people (Houston 2006, 7).

California's Folk Dance Federations

In May 1942, Henry "Buzz" Glass, another Chang dancer, proposed a federation model to organize the northern California folk dance clubs. Many club-sponsored festivals had occurred already during RIFD's short history in California. Glass believed that a federation would increase dancers' awareness of folk dance events and encourage choreographic standardization, so that dancers from different clubs would be able to dance together. The Folk Dance Federation of California was established with Glass as president in June 1942. Its membership included RIFD clubs, recreational Square Dance (RSD) clubs, and clubs that mixed RIFD and RSD (Casey 1981, 48–49).

In 1946, the federation created a permanent research committee chaired by Lucile Czarnowski. The purpose of the committee was to authenticate the origin of dances by identifying the first people who introduced the dances to RIFD, when and where the dances were introduced, and whether the dances were composed by choreographers or done in social settings. The research committee determined which dances should be taught at federation events, and it published hundreds of dance descriptions in the series *Folk Dances from Near and Far.* Chang's wrote the first set of dances descriptions for this series (Casey 1981, 48–49).

Katherine Jett (later Barnes) attempted to consolidate southern California folk dance clubs as early as 1941. Her efforts led to the Westwood Co-operative Folk Dancers in 1945. In 1946, the Westwood Co-operative Folk Dancers and other RIFD groups in southern California formed the Folk Dance Federation of California, South, with Allen Pelton as president. By 1947, the southern section had a membership of 65 RIFD groups and RSD groups, plus 17 nationality groups. The southern federation collaborated with the northern federation, and every year the two federations organized a statewide festival, which alternated between the two regions. The federations' first statewide festival was held in Ojai, California in May 1947 (Casey 1981, 49–50).

RIFD flourished in California under the federation model. The influx of new dancers sometimes caused problems, though, because the newcomers could not always keep up with long-time dancers who demanded more complex dances. Some clubs held multiple weekly dances catering to different skill levels. The best dancers often formed exhibition groups and performed at charity events, hospitals, churches, temples, schools, and folk festivals (Casey 1981, 47). RIFD festivals and summer camps, many of which were organized by the federations, welcomed dancers of all abilities. Festivals and camps were not only places to have fun in an immersive multisensory environment that combined dance, music, song, crafts, and food; they also gave teachers new material to take back to their clubs, and some even offered college or university credit (Shay 2008, 88).

Evening dance party at the 2009 Stockton Folk Dance Camp at University of the Pacific in Stockton, California. Author's archives.

World War II–1960s

The dances introduced to RIFD came from folk dance societies and organizations, RIFD club and federation publications, manuals by and for physical education teachers, nationality group performances, immigrants who led workshops for folk dancers, folk dancers who attended immigrants' social events, and folk dancers who learned dances overseas. A few professional choreographers composed folk dances specifically for RIFD, but a large percentage of the early dances were European social dances or ballroom dances. The majority of these dances were partner dances for heterosexual couples (Houston 2006, 8). Most dances lasted about three minutes, due to the technology of 78 rpm phonograph records (Shay 2008, 87).

Improvements in record manufacturing and heightened interest in ethnic records after World War II helped RIFD clubs in areas without musicians. It was difficult to find a soloist or band that could play the range of instruments and styles necessary for an international dance evening. After the war, three record companies captured most of the RIFD market for 78 rpm records: Folk Dancer, Folkraft, and Imperial Records. Victor and Columbia also sold a large number of records. In the 1950s, Folkraft, which targeted RIFD dancers, RSD dancers and schoolteachers, took the lead in record sales. Frank Kaltman and Dan Wolfert started Folkraft in New Jersey in 1946, and Rickey Holden, RIFD teacher and RSD caller, joined the company in 1951 (Houston 2006, 4–5). In the 1950s, the RSD and RIFD communities overlapped more than in the following decade. Some RIFD records featured American Square Dance calls, some RIFD clubs used RSD records, and some RSD clubs used RIFD records to supplement Round Dance, the couple dances in between group dances.

At first, most RIFD dances were done to a variety of tunes. Increasingly, though, folk dance teachers realized that if they built a dance around a catchy tune, they could sell records and make additional profit when they taught at clubs and camps. Increasingly, dancers needed to have the correct music in order to do a dance. Some RIFD enthusiasts believed that the standardization of dances with specific tunes killed the spirit of the dances. Others enjoyed the predictability and experienced a sense of accomplishment when they completed a dance, exactly as it had been taught and, to the correct tune.

The RIFD movement expanded in several directions, very quickly, after World War II. An American folk dancer named Nat Brown, stationed in London during the war, popularized RIFD and laid the groundwork for the Society for International Folk Dancing in London. Nibro and the Keithleys brought RIFD to Japan, and, in 1956, Earl Buckley, general secretary of the Tokyo YMCA, convinced the U.S. State Department and the Japanese newspaper chain *Asahi Shimbun* to sponsor a RIFD tour. Thousands of people across Japan learned RIFD from the Hermans, Nelda Guerrero Drury (a teacher from Mexico who introduced some of the first Mexican dances to RIFD dancers), Ralph Page, and Jane Farwell (a recreation leader who organized some of the first RIFD camps and created the Folklore Village in Wisconsin). In 1958 and the early 1960s, Rickey Holden also taught folk dancing in Japan as part of his world tours, which introduced RIFD and RSD to many nations (Houston 2006, 7).

In the United States, RIFD in the 1950s experienced a wave of foreign-born teachers and American-born teachers who wanted to specialize in a particular nation or region. Specialist folk dance communities began to take root. Some of these groups evolved within RIFD, inspired by a teacher who made a tremendous impression on the community. Other groups developed separate from RIFD, inspired by political events or popular culture, but the communities were similar enough in structure and spirit that the dances and dancers overlapped. Overall, the style of dancing shifted from partner dances to nonpartner dances in serpentine or circle formations. The majority of participants continued to be middle-class people of European descent, many of them associated with the burgeoning counterculture, some of them socialist or communist sympathizers.

RIFD gained a large Jewish following in New York City, where Fred Berk began an Israeli folk dance movement after the State of Israel was established in 1948. Before Berk, RIFD dancers only knew a handful of Jewish dances, mostly from Beliajus. Berk, an Austrian-born Jew who had studied modern dance in Germany, and his wife, Katya Delakova, began teaching Jewish folk dances and Palestinian folk dances at the 92nd Street Y in 1947. In the early 1950s, the 92nd Street Y became the American home for Israeli folk dance. In *Converging Movements: Modern Dance and Jewish Culture at the 92nd Street Y*, dance historian Naomi Jackson summarized,

> At the Y, Israeli folk dance symbolized Israel and a unified Jewish people, with dances like Berk's *Holiday in Israel* (1952) idealizing "the land," rustic simplicity, and the joy of existence. Such a view suited the desire on the part of many American Jews to retain a strong cultural connection with Israel without necessarily making aliyah (settling there). At the Y, young Jews could passionately experience the "Israeli spirit" and rejoice in the euphoria of the creation of a state that assured them that they were no longer members of an uprooted, persecuted people. At the same time, they celebrated from a comfortable, middle-class distance in the well-maintained halls of the Y, confirming postwar Jew's rootedness to American society and their own successful cultural life within America. (2000, 14–15)

Berk's dance compositions focused on the pioneer spirit. They combined modern dance with various dance traditions from places where Jewish people had settled, such as Eastern Europe and Yemen. The modern dance tradition of going barefoot carried over into Israeli dance, influencing some folk dancers to go barefoot for regular RIFD sessions (Houston 2006, 8).

In 1950, Beliajus taught eight Kolos (a nonpartner dance common in present-day Croatia and Serbia) at Stockton Folk Dance Camp, initiating a period in RIFD known as Kolomania. The Hermans introduced more Kolos to Stockton Folk Dance Camp in 1951. The same year, John Filcich started the Kolo Festival in San Francisco to raise money for Beliajus, who was suffering from an illness. The festival became an annual event over Thanksgiving weekend. Armenian dances swept RIFD concurrently, popularized by Frances Ajoian, who later inspired folk dance teachers Tom Bozigian and Gary and Susan Lind-Sinanian. Olga Veloff Sandolowich and Michel Cartier went to Bulgaria and brought back dances from professional companies. Larisa Lucaci taught Romanian dances and inspired Sunni Bloland, brothers Mihai and Alexandru David, and Nico Hilferink (Houston 2006, 8–9).

In the early 1960s, RIFD clubs did a variety of dances. Bulgarian folk dance teacher Yves Moreau recalled, "We would do in an evening Israeli, Balkan, Russian, Greek, Mexican, line dance, couple dances, everything. That was certainly one of the things then—international folk dance was truly international" (interview by author, August 7, 2009). Folk dance enthusiast Kristina Efimenko, who began folk dancing as a teenager in Phoenix, Arizona in the 1960s, stated,

> One of the things I liked about folk dancing was that you didn't have to know the dance before you could participate. They said, "Just grab a hand," and they would pull you this way and that way, and eventually your feet would catch on. Some people didn't want to do it that way, so they would stand behind the line and take minute notes: so many steps to the right, so many steps to the left—that kind of thing and in special dance notation. But I never did that. I just joined in. (Interview by author, January 15, 2009)

Recreational folk dancers knew the national origin of dances, but they often trivialized or ignored the dances' original cultural context. It was only important that the dances were fun and international (Laušević 2007, 161).

State-Sponsored Folk Ensembles

In the mid-1950s, national folk music and dance ensembles from the Soviet Union and Eastern Bloc began to tour North America, drawing folk dancers' attention to this part of the world. Tanec, from Macedonia, and Kolo, from Serbia, were the first to arrive in 1956 (Shay 2008, 90). Folk dance historian Anthony Shay recalled when the Soviet Union's Moiseyev Dance Company came to the United States in 1958,

> We had never seen precision dancing done by so many individuals together. . . . They showed them first on the Ed Sullivan show. . . . Americans, millions of them, saw this group. Contrary to the image that the State Department and Hollywood had created together, here were 100 wholesome, happy, all-smiling, all-dancing, all-the-time group that were just over the top. America was absolutely transfixed. (Interview by author, December 27, 2008)

Most touring ensembles were subsidized by communist governments and used fun-in-the-village peasant themes (Shay 2002, 9). Professional choreographers modified folk dances from their original context by adding rhythmic complexity, intricate footwork, kaleidoscopic spatial patterns, and stylized uniformity such as 90-degree knee angles and pointed toes. Shay reflected, upon seeing the Moiseyev Dance Company, "Suddenly, everything that we had performed in our exhibitions appeared quaint and inadequate" (2008, 90).

Some folk dance enthusiasts recognized the opportunity to use folk dance as art and distanced themselves from recreational clubs to start or join exhibition groups. These groups acquired dancers through auditions, rehearsed intensively, performed onstage for audiences, and often had live musicians. Some of the most well-known International Folk Dance ensembles were the AMAN Folk Ensemble, of Los Angeles; the Westwind Ensemble, of San Francisco and Los Angeles; the Ethnic Dance Theatre, of Minneapolis; the Komenka Dance Company, of New Orleans; Khadra, of San Francisco; the AVAZ International Dance Theatre, of Los Angeles; and Mandala, of Boston (Shay 2008, 90). Many IFD groups were linked to colleges or universities either as a physical education teacher's side project or fully integrated into curriculum (notably the Duquesne University Tamburitzans and Brigham Young University's folk ensembles).

The state-sponsored national folk dance ensembles brought a new wave of teachers and dances to North America. RIFD clubs sometimes organized workshops or parties with the ensembles after their performances. Yves Moreau remembered, "These people would come and do a performance, and we'd dance with them. Michael Herman would teach them a Virginia Reel or something. It was a nice exchange"

AVAZ International Dance Theatre performing Katanka, a dance from eastern Serbia, choreographed by Anthony Shay. Photographer D. Young. Courtesy of Anthony Shay.

(interview by author, August 7, 2009). Shay, a member of the Gandy Dancers when Kolo came in 1956, elaborated, "We learned every choreography from [Kolo] the dancers taught us. It was amazing, because we actually thought they were all real folk dances. It never occurred to us that many of them were someone's creation" (interview by author, December 27, 2008). With limited knowledge about eastern Europe, most folk dancers in the U.S. accepted that what they saw onstage was exactly how foreigners danced in social settings.

Going Balkan

In the 1960s and 1970s, a popular theme in the RIFD movement was the romanticization of peasant lifeRIFD enthusiasts believed that the sense of community lacking in American society could be found by going to ethnic events or, even better, to the source. The Balkans appealed to folk dancers because self-sufficient agriculturalist villages still existed, and the characteristic circular or serpentine hand-holding nonpartner dances suggested to folk dancers an ideal egalitarian community. In these dances, the entire group worked together as a unit by stepping and swaying with the same momentum. To RIFD enthusiasts, the term "Balkan dance" generally encompassed dances from Bulgaria, Croatia, Greece, Macedonia, Romania, and Serbia.

The Balkan dance craze gained momentum when a few folk dance teachers traveled to the Balkans in the 1950s and 1960s to collect dances. Richard Crum, who grew up in a Romanian neighborhood in St. Paul, Minnesota, is given credit for promoting the Balkan movement early on. He initially taught Slovenian couple dances but then switched to nonpartner dances from Croatia, Romania, and Serbia (Houston 2006, 12–13). After Sandolowich and Cartier, Yves Moreau went to Bulgaria in the late 1960s and launched his RIFD career at a Kolo Festival in San Francisco.

In the early 1970s, folk dancers began to travel regularly to the Balkans to do the festival circuit. Moreau explained, "You'd go for a summer and find out where all the festivals were in Macedonia, Bulgaria, and you'd just go from one to the other. The same people kept bumping into each other throughout the summer" (interview by author, August 7, 2009). Increased travel led to folk dance group vacations organized by RIFD teachers. In the Balkans, RIFD enthusiasts experienced both improvised and choreographed dances at social events and festivals. When these dancers returned to the U.S., the normal RIFD sessions to recorded music did not offer the same experience. Some folk dancers stopped dancing altogether, some remained in RIFD, and others diverged from RIFD and formed a Balkan dance community.

Many Balkan dance enthusiasts learned to play Balkan instruments, cook Balkan food, and speak Balkan languages. Some made *kavals,* or end-blown flutes, out of PVC pipes for informal playing, whereas others created professional bands such as Zlatne Uste, a Balkan brass band consisting entirely of Americans. The Balkans was more than a hobby; the region represented decades of scholarly commitment or musical practice, frequent travel, and a community of likeminded enthusiasts. Balkan camps appeared where participants shared dance and music knowledge and created idealized village experiences. In such settings, the ultimate dance experience entailed adapting and improvising dance sequences to live music, sometimes for more than an hour. Individuals were able to exit and reenter the dance at any

The Cope family of San Francisco, active in the recreational Balkan community, celebrate daughter Lacey's imminent trip to Bulgaria for college (see http://lacey. thecopes.com). Lacey is leading the dance on the far left. Several party attendees had participated in the 2009 Mendocino Balkan Music and Dance Workshop a few weeks prior. Author's archives.

time, taking breaks for food and beverages, similar to an actual social dance event in the Balkans.

The 1970s and Beyond

Most RIFD clubs have concentrated on Balkan dance since the late 1960s, but several other kinds of recreational folk dance (and related) groups emerged after 1970. In the late 1970s, Judith and Kálmán Magyar started the Hungarian Tánchaz (dance house) movement. In 1980, Gordon Tracie launched the Scandinavian dance movement with the first Scandia Camp Mendocino. Later that decade, Richard Powers started the Vintage Dance (historical ballroom dance) movement and Roy Hilburn introduced folk dancers to Cajun dances and Cajun dancers to RIFD. Pat Shaw's original choreography sparked a Modern English Country Dance movement in the 1970s, and the Jane Austen movies of the 1990s inspired countless people to learn the old Playford dances as well as the newer English dances. Also in the 1990s, the Country-Western and Line Dance movement produced hundreds of dances. Many RIFD enthusiasts participated in CWLD events, but the dances did not gain a foothold in RIFD club repertoire (Houston 2006, 14).

A new generation of Balkan music and dance enthusiasts emerged in the early 21st century, separate from the RIFD community. For the most part, these musicians and dancers were the children of the people who had started the movement in the late 1960s and early 1970s. Several participants at the 2009 Mendocino Balkan Music and Dance Workshop told the author that youth stayed involved in the group because of the good music and a solidarity that is difficult to find in other social groups. Furthermore, the Balkan community imitates life in the Balkans, where social events integrate different generations. Most of the young Balkan enthusiasts grew up going to Balkan camps and ethnic events with their parents.

Sunni Bloland leads an RIFD session at the Ashkenaz Music and Dance Community Center in Berkeley, California (circa 1970). Courtesy of Sunni Bloland.

RIFD membership declined after the late 1960s, and the community began to gray without an influx of young dancers. Some dancers blamed this on the dictatorial nature of some RIFD teachers. Others pointed to the music. In the late 1960s, cassette tapes facilitated music pirating, and copies upon copies of tapes resulted in subpar sound quality (Houston 2006, 8). Many folk dancers also blamed the cessation of folk dance programs in physical education. Sunni Bloland, former folk dance teacher at University of California at Berkeley, summarized the height and decline of RIFD on her campus as follows,

> Kids would come down, hundreds of them, to dance on a Friday night. . . . It was wonderful. It was a time when folk dancing was something new, was attractive. People liked the community, the feeling of community, the holding hands. You didn't have to have a partner. It was an extraordinary time in our society. . . . Then the plague came and wiped it out. It wasn't anymore to be seen. We fell off the edge of the Earth and there was no more folk dancing. Don't ask me why. . . . I said, "Where are these hundreds of students I used to have?" No. I had eight or 10 or 15. . . . Finished. It's dead. It's gone. . . . So that's the way I ended it all. . . . The time changed. Ballroom dancing was there to take its place. I had a huge class of social dancing: Fox Trot, Tango, Waltz. (Interview, August 1, 2009)

In the 1980s, other dance forms readily replaced folk dances in physical education settings, distancing students (and potential RIFD enthusiasts) from the knowledge necessary to understand and appreciate an RIFD festival or club event.

7

Modern Western Square Dance

A recreational Square Dance (RSD) movement took off shortly after World War II. Factors that led up to the movement included Cecil Sharp's "discovery" of the Running Set and increased scholarly interest in rural American dance forms, polite society's opposition to dance halls, a surge in adult group recreation, rural retreats where city dwellers experienced rural community dances, Henry Ford's old-fashioned dance revival, Lloyd Shaw's research on cowboy dances, Square Dance records, and fairs and festivals that featured Square Dance. Slowly at first, American rural dances began to seep into schools and colleges. Youth group leaders seeped into youth groups, schools, and colleges. Some adults also caught the Square Dance bug and formed RSD clubs and exhibition groups.

Many schoolteachers, who were pressured or required to know Square Dance for physical education classes, traveled as callers during the summer months to call at folk festivals. In the 1930s, Herb Greggerson, Ed Gilmore, and Les Gotcher were among the few full-time RSD callers who traveled year-round to call dances in different places (Mayo 2003, 21). Greggerson traveled continuously from 1938 to 1944. Bob Brundage, one of the first RSD callers in New England along with his brother, Al, remembers Greggerson as the first caller who brought American rural dances from outside of New England to New England, "The first time we were exposed to any sort of Western style dancing was when Herb Greggerson, from Ruidoso, New

Mexico, came through on a tour . . . and taught us things that we had never heard of before" (interview by author, March 2, 2009).

During and after World War II, Square Dance was more than a fun recreational activity; it was a symbol and expression of American pride. Callers who worked at or visited United Service Organizations (USOs) planted the seeds for RSD in several countries, including Australia, England, Germany, and Japan. By the mid-1950s, RSD was established in American schools and youth groups, and RSD clubs existed in several countries. RSD in other countries followed the trends that happened in the United States, and callers in non-English-speaking countries did not translate the terminology; they used the same calls as American callers.

Early RSD manuals covered a wide range of dance forms and topics related to organizing dances and calling. Two of the most comprehensive books were Lloyd Shaw's *Cowboy Dances* (1939) and *The Round Dance Book* (1948). Calling was addressed in such resources as *Square Dance Callers Instruction Course* (1949), by Ed Gilmore, *Square Dances of Today and How to Teach Them* (1950), by Richard Kraus, and *The Square Dance Caller (1950)*, by Rickey Holden. Many resources were collections of dances, such as *Honor Your Partner* (1938), by Carl Hertzog, *Herb's Blue Bonnet Calls* (1939), by Herb Greggerson, and *The Newest and Latest Square Dance Singing Calls* (1953), by Cal Golden. Margot Mayo, leader of New York City's American Square Dance Group, published *The American Square Dance* (1943) with dances from different regions as well as play-party games.

Square Dance radio programs and records helped drive the RSD movement. In 1944, Henry Ford started a Saturday night dance program on the Blue Network. His Early American Music program featured dancing master Benjamin Lovett as the caller, and the live orchestra consisted of accordion, dulcimer, cymbalum, bass viol, and fiddle. Michael Herman gave the program "top billing" in *The Folk Dancer*, stating, "Any group listening to the program can get up and do the Quadrilles, Schottisches, Galops, Polkas, and Waltzes" (June 1944, 4:6, 14). Ford was dedicated to refined 19th century ballroom dances, but his radio show and dance records (produced by his friend Thomas Edison) helped the RSD movement indirectly by popularizing Quadrilles. Then, exhibition groups such as Ed Larkin's Old Time Contra Dancers, Herb Greggerson's Blue Bonnet Set, and Lloyd Shaw's Cheyenne Mountain Dancers showed city dwellers that rural dances could be smooth and elegant.

In the 1940s, small RSD events usually featured a fiddler (who was often the caller) or a pianist, but larger events often had a full orchestra with accordion, banjo, bass fiddle, fiddle, guitar, and piano (Dawson and Bell 1961, 7). After 1950, live music gave way to records. Folkraft and C.P. MacGregor were the earliest record companies to regularly produce RSD records. Fenton "Jonesy" Jones and Les Gotcher called for C.P. MacGregor in the late 1940s. "Doc" Alambaugh created Windsor Records in 1949. More companies came in the 1950s (Mayo 2003, 11). In 1956, RCA Victor issued *Let's Square Dance*, a five-album set prepared by Richard Kraus that was used in physical education classrooms. It included some of the most popular RSD dances of the era: "Red River Valley," "Comin' Round the Mountain," "Dip and Dive," "When Johnny Comes Marching Home," and "Hot Time in the Old Town Tonight" (Rossoff 1977, 16).

Square Dance Clubs in the McCarthy Era

Rural community dances only used about 15 to 20 figures or calls, and these figures were repeated across dances (Mayo 2003, 27). Lessons were not required, because the dancers learned the figures in a walk-through beforehand or by watching other couples during the dance. City dwellers originally learned these kinds dances for their own recreation. Dance historians often use the term "Traditional Square Dance" to differentiate these early dance forms from Square Dance forms for enthusiasts who did not grow up with the dances as part of their small town life. In the 1930s and early 1940s, for RSD, the club structure was not as popular as Saturday night dances or informal gatherings in people's living rooms or basements. Children often were present. Then, in the late 1940s, city dwellers grew tired of the original dances; they demanded more novelty and variety, RSD choreography began to changed, and official clubs with bylaws and memberships took hold.

Changes to RSD inspired Square Dance enthusiasts to create clubs and hold lessons, in order to teach new dancers the basics. When dancers graduated from the lessons, they were allowed to dance with a club. The club-based Square Dance (sometimes called Modern Square Dance or Contemporary Square Dance) movement took hold first in southern California, centered around caller Bob Osgood. Osgood called dances throughout the United States and in several countries, consulted for dance scenes in Hollywood movies, organized callers' workshops and festivals, produced numerous records, and published the widely distributed *Sets in Order* magazine for 37 years. By 1949, there were nearly 200 RSD clubs in southern California (Mayo 2003, 38). By the late 1950s, RSD clubs had spread across North America and overseas. Many of these clubs followed the new style of Modern Square Dance.

Some RSD clubs were led by a caller. Other clubs were led by dancers, with leadership roles often filled jointly by married couples. Many clubs were for married couples, but there were also clubs for the general public, singles, children, teens, and the elderly. Clubs usually met weekly or twice a month, and the dance evenings frequently included a potluck dinner and an after-party at someone's home (Mayo 2003, 37). As the number of clubs and callers grew, RSD enthusiasts formed federations and associations to help organize their activity (Dosado.com, the Western Square Dancing website, provides an up-to-date list of clubs, federations, and associations). RSD enthusiasts even built Square Dance halls in some cities, and these halls usually came equipped with a kitchen to support potlucks.

Some of the California RSD clubs joined the Folk Dance Federation of California (North and South), but, in the late 1940s, southern California callers established a separate federation for RSD clubs. The move was in part political. Shortly thereafter, several RSD callers also withdrew their affiliation with the Stockton Folk Dance Camp at the University of the Pacific in Stockton, California. When Lawton Harris founded the camp on the Methodist campus in 1948, he specified that the program was to include include as much American dance as International Folk Dance. In RIFD, however, eastern European dances were becoming popular, and some patriotic RSD callers and dancers viewed these so-called communist dances as un-American. In fact, more than once in the McCarthy era, government officials went to Stockton Folk Dance Camp to investigate potential communist activity (Jerry Helt and John Filcich, interview by author, August 6, 2009). The rift between RSD and RIFD continued to widen in the decades ahead. Specifically, MWSD attracted more politically conservative, individuals of Anglo-Saxon Protestant heritage, many of whom were former military servicemen and servicewomen. In comparison, RIFD attracted more liberal counterculture supporters, the type of people who were known to skinny dip at dance camps and march in protests.

Square Dance television shows and movies helped drive the RSD club movement, as well. The television was new technology in the 1940s and 1950s, and it quickly replaced the radio as the dominant form of in-home entertainment. As the television seeped into rural areas, neighbors who previously socialized on Saturday nights at the town hall dance instead met in someone's living room for a more sedentary kind of socialization (sometimes there was only one television in the community). The variety show *ABC Barn Dance* (1949) was a spinoff of the radio show *National Barn Dance*. *The Old American Barn Dance* (1953) was very popular. Square Dance movies from the first decade of Western Square Dance included *Hollywood Barn Dance* (1947), *Square Dance Jubilee* (1949), *The Arkansas Swing* (1949), and *Square Dance Katy* (1950) (Giordano 2007, 2:124).

In the early 1950s, a typical RSD club evening was a mixture of group dances and couple dances were known as Round Dance, because the dancers traveled in a circle around the room. Old-time couple dances such as the Polka, Schottische, Two-Step, Varsovienne, and Waltz gave the dancers a break from the longer group dances. The Waltz and represented Two-Step 95 percent of couple dances in RSD clubs by the early 1960s (Hamilton 1962, 8). Some RSD clubs borrowed couple dances from RIFD, but this practice became increasingly uncommon as the Modern Western Square Dance (MWSD) dominated RSD clubs and RIFD clubs pushed out couple dances in favor of non-partner dances from Israel and the Balkans.

At RSD clubs, group dances included square dances for four couples, circle dances, partner-changing mixers, and longways dances for lines of couples. Longways dances mainly happened in New England, where these dances had been part of the local tradition for centuries. Most RSD clubs in other parts of the country did not have the same interest in longways dances (Holden 1956, iv).

Choreographic Changes

Modern Square Dance primarily evolved from Visiting Couple dances, which were popular in rural communities in the west, and were advocated by Lloyd Shaw and Bob Osgood. The Visiting Couple dances had numerous variations. They evolved from New England dances, southern Appalachian dances, and other dances during westward expansion. The dancers' positions were numbered counterclockwise from Couple 1, who faced away from the musicians. Couples 1 and 3 were the head couples, and Couples 2 and 4 were the side couples. In the 1940s, Visiting Couple dances done by RSD enthusiasts in southern California included Spanish Caballero, Golden Slippers, Marching Thru Georgia, Duck for the Oyster, Wring Out the Old Dish Rag, The Basket, Grapevine, and the Waltz Quadrille (Mayo 2003, 4).

A Visiting Couple dance began with honors (bows and curtseys) and an opening figure for the entire group. Then, Couple 1 danced a figure with Couple 2, and all the dancers danced a brief subchorus. Then Couple 1 repeated the figure with Couple 3, and, again, the dancers danced a subchorus. After Couple 1 visited Couple 4, with the subchorus, the entire group danced a longer break or a chorus. Next, Couple 2 repeated the same sequence as Couple 1, starting from their position in the set and visiting counterclockwise. Then Couple 3 danced the same sequence. After Couple 4 visited around the set, the caller called a finish, or closing figure, for the entire group. The main figure always stayed the same, and it often took the name of the song title. The caller sometimes gave the dance variety by substituting different openings, subchoruses, choruses, and finishes (Shaw 1939, 30, 147–164; Owens 1949, 37).

Modern Square Dance preserved the multi-dance tip structure characteristic of rural community dances in the West. Each dance in the tip went to a different tune, separated by a pause. Usually, a two-part tip consisted of a patter call followed by a singing call, and a three-part tip consisted of a singing call, patter call, and another singing call. In a singing call, the caller matched his or her (but usually his) voice to the tune of the song, and then he sang the actual song lyrics during refrains as the dancers completed a figure. The patter call, on the other hand, was done to a variety of tunes, because the caller called in a monotone chant. The caller gave the instructions and then chanted patter, or doggerel, to finish a rhyme as the dancers completed a figure. The extra words differentiated patter calling from prompting. A prompter was someone who only gave movement commands, whereas a caller usually sang or rhymed in addition to giving movement commands (Mayo 2003, 3–4; Owens 1949, 19–22).

The spread of public address systems and microphones in the late 1940s enabled new choreographic possibilities, because the dancers were able to hear the caller more clearly (Mayo 2003, 6). Suddenly, the dancers who stood in the back of the room were able to respond to actual calls; they did not have to rely on memorizing the dances or trying to interpret muffled intonations. Callers began to experiment with the choreography. The first choreographic modifications were simple. Instead of calling for one couple, callers called for opposite couples. While Couple 1 was visiting Couple 2, Couple 3 simultaneously visited Couple 4. The caller either called the same figure or different figures for the active couples (Mayo 2003, 5–6; Dawson and Bell 1961, 10).

Next, callers experimented with traveling patterns and formations. Dancers no longer were limited to visiting the other couples around the set and returning home. In the Goalpost pattern, for example, two inactive couples stood as human goalposts, and the active couples danced figures through and around them. For the Grid pattern, popularized by Greggerson, four-couple sets oriented themselves back-to-back with other four-couple sets, and the caller moved couples into neighboring sets, traveling across the room. The objective was to find new pathways and formations to make the dances more interesting and reduce the amount of inactivity, because the dancers were not interested in standing around; they wanted to move (Mayo 2003).

Pathway experimentation inspired callers to create new calls, in order to have more ways to get dancers from place to place. Before this point, if a caller wanted to introduce a new call, he or she had to create an entire dance around it. Callers soon realized that they could substitute new calls, different calls, or series of calls, into preexisting choreography. The calls would be successful as long as the dancers were in the correct positions to start the chorus, which took them back to their starting positions. Callers began to invent longer compound calls, which combined preexisting calls under a new name. Some of these calls were very complex and changed the dancers' positions within the set (Mayo 2003, 52–53).

Choreographic innovation happened slowly at first. In the early 1950s, dancers were able to learn enough calls to participate effectively in about six to 10 lessons. In those days, the most popular calls included Allemande Left, Grand Right and Left, Promenade, Swing, Dos-A-Dos, Docey-doe, Do Paso, Right and Left Thru, Ladies Chain and See Saw, Star, All Around (Left Hand Lady), California Twirl and Circle (Mayo 2003, 27). The terms Dos-A-Dos (from the East) Docey-doe (from Texas) were pronounced the same, which created confusion when callers traveled between regions. Dos-A-Dos was from

French and meant "back-to-back," as two dancers walked in a circle around each other back-to-back. Docey-doe, on the other hand, came from Spanish and meant "two-by-two." For the Docey-doe, dancers grabbed hands with their partners and turned, grabbed hands with their corners (the adjacent dancers) and turned, and then the men put an arm around their partner's waist and guide ed the women to the home positions her home (Durlacher 1949, 23; Anderson 1950, vii). Callers at Shaw's 1949 summer school resolved that Docey-doe would be renamed Dos Paso (later Do Paso) to honor its Texan heritage (Mayo 2003, 7, 47).

By the early 1960s, callers recognized the need for methods to to manage RSD choreography beyond the existing, pre-choreographed patters that were delivered the same way every time. The first books about choreographic management were *The Keys to Calling Square Dances* (1961), by Bob Dawson and Don Bell, and *Instant Hash* (1962), by Rickey Holden and Lloyd Litman. At first, hash (also known as chopsuey, succotash, or scrambled eggs) was a type of novelty dance. It entailed combining parts of memorized routines in ways that were unpredictable to the dancers (Rossoff 1977, 17–19). Hash caught on very quickly. By the late 1960s, the term "hot hash" was adopted for calls executed at a rapid pace where call sequences did not immediately resolve dancers' positions within the set, and the term "hash calling" came to describe any type of calling that produced continuous movement (Allan Hurst, e-mail to author, November 12, 2010).

In the 1960s, RSD increasingly distanced itself from its rural origins, and callers and dancers began to define their activity as Modern Western Square Dance (MWSD). In *Step by Step Through Modern Square Dance History* (2003), Jim Mayo stated that the fundamental attribute of MWSD was "the changing of the dance routine as it is being danced" (2003, x). In other words, dancers were not able to predict the choreography and had to listen to the caller. Furthermore, callers no longer had to memorize full dances. Some dancers grew frustrated, thinking that they had to memorize every new call in order to not embarrass themselves at a dance. After all, it only took one person to make an entire square break down, and then everyone in the broken set had to return to their original positions and wait for the caller to bring the other sets back home, in order for the broken set to resume. To avoid meltdowns, dancers preferred to dance with people of the same skill level. Most RSD clubs welcomed anyone who graduated from the lessons, but some clubs were more exclusive and regulated membership by using an invitation-only model or meeting in private locations, (Mayo 2003, 85).

MWSD grew rapidly in the 1970s. There were over 1,500 calls by 1976, and the number more than doubled within a decade (Mayo 2003, 63). Callers generally agreed that dancers could learn the fundamental calls in about 30 weeks, at a rate of about one and a half calls per class. Some dancers who wanted even more variety studied All Position Dancing (APD), which relaxed the traditional constraints associated with gender (Mayo 2003, 118). Callers continued to develop new calls, novelty dances, and choreographic management methods throughout the decade. At the Massachusetts Institute of Technology (MIT), Clark Baker brought modern technology into the mix in 1976 when he wrote the first Square Dance computer program to figure out how to combine calls in new ways (Mayo 2003, 133–134). Other MWSD computer programs followed.

CALLERLAB and Conventions

MWSD appealed to many people who did not consider themselves dancers, because simply walking memorized patterns was enough to get through a dance. Some callers felt that the quality of the dancing was diminishing with MWSD; the dancers were moving on top of the music, rather than with the music. There was little time to work on gracefulness, though, when dancers' primary concern was keeping up with the calls. The nation's leading MWSD callers felt that they needed a national organization that could filter good calls from awkward calls, train callers to teach dance etiquette as well as calls, and create standardized list of calls known as dance programs (or levels). With dance programs, dancers anywhere in the world who graduated from the lessons would have the same knowledge and could dance together (Mayo 2003, 103).

In 1971, Bob Osgood and several of the nation's leading MWSD callers met to discuss CALLERLAB, the National Association of Square Dance Callers (later the International Association of Square Dance Callers). Aside from Osgood, the participants were Don Armstrong, Al Brundage, Marshall Flippo, Ed Gilmore, Lee Helsel, Bruce Johnson, Earl Johnston, Arnie Kronenberger, Frank Lane, Johnny LeClair, Joe Lewis, Bob Page, Dave Taylor, and Bob Van Antwerp. Ed Gilmore

MWSD with caller Rick Gittelman at the 2009 Tucson Area Square Dance Festival, sponsored by the Southern Arizona Callers and Cuers Association. Photo courtesy of David Lefton.

passed away that year, but he was involved in earlier planning meetings. In 1972, callers Jim Mayo, Jerry Helt, and Jerry Haag joined the group, and CALLERLAB became a permanent organization with an annual convention (Mayo 2003, 98–99). The majority of callers were men, and only one woman, Osa Mathews, was present at the first CALLERLAB convention in St. Louis, Missouri in 1974 (Mayo 2003, 103).

Over time, CALLERLAB created the following dance programs: Mainstream, Plus, Advanced, and Challenge, with sublevels for Advanced and Challenge. CALLERLAB evaluates all of its dance programs every three years and occasionally makes minor updates. Some callers also teach a program called Basic, which has the first 53 calls on the Mainstream list. Many Mainstream calls overlap with the calls used in rural community dances. The classes for each level take several months to complete, and a dancer must graduate from one dance program before moving onto the next dance program. (The CALLERLAB website, Callerlab.org, provides up-to-date information about the programs.) Not every MWSD caller is affiliated with CALLERLAB, but the advantages of membership include professional development through training and certification, copyright permission to use recorded music, and keeping up with the latest MWSD trends. Furthermore, many MWSD dancers demand that their callers teach the CALLERLAB dance programs, so that they can participate at large-scale conventions and festivals that use these programs (Clark Baker, CALLERLAB, n.d.; email to author, May 17, 2011; Rick Gittelman, interview by author, January 9, 2009).

The National Square Dance Convention, first held in Riverside, California in 1952, is the largest MWSD event. It attracts thousands of dancers from all over North America as well as abroad. The 1976 convention in Anaheim, California was a record year with nearly 40,000 participants. That year, the U.S. bicentennial, RSD celebrations were held across the nation to celebrate American heritage. The next largest attendance, approximately 31,000 dancers, occurred in 1983 (Mayo 2003, 127). The National Square Dance Convention divides rooms by dance program, so Mainstream dancers dance in Mainstream rooms, Plus dancers dance in Plus rooms or Mainstream rooms, and so on. The convention gives dancers the opportunity to dance to multiple callers, and callers change rooms in order to call for different groups of dancers.

Other MWSD conventions and festivals are organized by the CALLERLAB programs, as well, and some events cater to specific programs or interest groups. Regional Advanced/Challenge weekends, for example, enable dancers at the upper levels to concentrate on material that is not taught at most clubs. The majority of MWSD clubs in the United States dance at the Mainstream and Plus levels. In 1968, Ed Foote started the National Challenge Convention, and the annual event was renamed the Academy for Advanced and Challenge Enthusiasts in 2001. The National Singles Square Dance Convention began in 1970, organized by Single Square Dancers USA. The first GLBT (gay, lesbian, bisexual, transgendered) or gay MWSD club, the South Florida Mustangs, formed in 1980. By 1984, there were enough gay MWSD clubs to hold a National Gay Square Dance Convention (Mayo 2003, 105, 136). The largest European MWSD event is the international Plus, Advanced & Challenge Square Dance Convention (iPAC), held in Germany every two years since 1993. The first Australian National Square Dance Convention occurred in 1952, and the first All Japan Square Dance Convention occurred in 1961.

Round Dance, Contra Dance, Line Dance, and Clogging

CALLERLAB, which sets the standards and rules for affiliated callers and clubs, was a strong influence on MWSD club culture. The CALL-ERLAB model also informed parallel organizations, ROUNDALAB, the International Association of Round Dance Teachers, and CON-TRALAB, the International Association of Contra Callers. Round Dance teachers (also known as cuers) organized ROUNDALAB in 1976 to standardize vocabulary, train cuers, and establish phases (similar to CALLERLAB's dance programs). MWSD Contra Dance callers, who specialized in the New England longways sets, created CONTRA-LAB in 1986 for similar purposes. In the MWSD community, Contra Dance was never popular as regular square sets or couple dances.

Round Dance became very popular in the 1970s and 1980s, and specialist Round Dance clubs formed separate from MWSD clubs. Round Dance cuers were often married to MWSD callers, and some-times married couples worked together as cuers, taking turns. In the Round Dance phases, cuers teach figures to different rhythms, usu-ally beginning with the Waltz and Two-Step. Later, they introduce fig-ures from 20th century dances, such as the Cha-Cha, Rumba, Jive, Single Swing, West Coast Swing, Lindy, Hustle, Bolero, Slow Two-Step, Mambo, Salsa, Samba, Argentine Tango, Merengue, and Paso Doble (Round Dancing, n.d.). Many of these dances came from Latin America, and they were popularized by competitive ballroom dancing, as well as increased Latin American migration to the United States in the 1960s.

MWSD events almost always feature Round Dance, particularly if the event contains many married couples. Large events, such as the National Square Dance Convention, also feature Contra Dance, Line Dance, and Clogging. Some MWSD clubs incorporate these dance forms into their regular programs, as well, if there is a teacher and enough interest among the dancers. MWSD clubs use recorded mu-sic almost exclusively. Some dances are tied to specific songs, but the highly improvisatory four-couple squares can be done to a wide range of music, including 21st century pop songs.

In the 1970s, Grant F. Longley, a junior college athletic director, in-troduced Line Dance to MWSD through his New, Modern Ballroom

Dance program. The program consisted of nonpartner dances, including the Hokey-Pokey and Israeli and Greek circle dances (not considered New, Modern Ballroom Dances) to supplement the individualized, scattered nonpartner dances (Longley 1977, 2–3). During the Line Dance craze of the 1950s and 1960s, a caller or prompter gave the commands to dancers, and the dancers faced the same direction, scattered throughout the room, and rarely made physical contact with one another. Some dances were unpredictable, and other dances used repetitive figures. Despite Longley's efforts, Line Dance was not common at MWSD conventions and festivals until the 1990s. Line Dance rarely occurred at MWSD clubs, but many people found MWSD through Line Dance at country western bars. (Bill Eyler, e-mail to author, November 15, 2010).

The Country Western Dance craze of the 1980s and 1990s helped revive Line Dance. The movie *Urban Cowboy* (1980), with John Travolta, is usually credited for sparking interest in Country Western Dance. In 1992, Billy Ray Cyrus's recording of "Achy Breaky Heart" sold over 11 million copies, and it started a Line Dance craze to country western music. Country Line Dance enthusiasts formed clubs, and their dress code was Western attire. The men wore bolo ties, belt buckles, jeans, and vests. The women wore fringed shirts, jeans, or frilly dresses. Both sexes wore cowboy hats and cowboy boots. The magazine *Country Dance Lines* (1984–2000) identified thousands of Country Line Dance instructors in numerous countries, described over 5,000 dances, and reached about 22,000 subscribers (Giordano 2007, 2:291–293).

In the 1990s, country western bars typically featured Country Line Dance, MWSD, and Round Dance. Popular couple dances included the Blue Rose, Cowboy Cha Cha (or Traveling Cha Cha), El Paso, Kansas City Four Corners, Sweetheart Scottische, and Wooden Nickel (Giordano 2007, 2:293). Some MWSD clubs held their weekly gatherings at country western bars, despite the fact that MWSD had the reputation of being a sober activity (drinking caused squares to break down). At first, many gay MWSD clubs met at gay country western bars, sometimes because MWSD halls did not have enough space with all the preexisting groups, and sometimes because conservative dance hall schedulers believed that MWSD should be a heterosexual activity for married couples (Bill Eyler, interview by author, March 2, 2009).

Clogging happens at large MWSD events and in some clubs, but the Clog dancers who cross over to MWSD generally participate in separate Clogging activities separate from MWSD. The television show *Hee Haw* drew nationwide attention to Clogging beginning in 1969, and a Tap Dance revival in the late 1970s inspired many people to take up Clogging. In the 1970s, Clog dancers across the nation used different terminology, which caused confusion when people from different regions tried to dance together. Roberta Adams founded the *Double Toe Times* magazine in 1978, was one of the first moves to unify the Clogging community. Jeff Driggs took over the magazine in 1998.

In recreational settings, Clog instructors either teach their own dances or prechoreographed dances that they learn from published cuesheets, festivals, workshops, or conventions. C.L.O.G., the National Clogging Organization, provides a National Dance List with cuesheets on its Web site, Clog.org. There are three major sanctioning organizations that host clogging competitions nationally: C.L.O.G.'s National Clogging and Hoedown Council (NCHC), America's Clog-

Clogging at the 2009 National Square Dance Convention, in Long Beach, California. Author's archives.

ging Hall of Fame (ACHF) , and the Clogging Champions of America (CCA). CCA has attracted the largest following among the more contemporary styles of clogging, as seen on *America's Best Dance Crew, So You Think You Can Dance,* and *America's Got Talent.* NCHC and ACHF offering a variety of competition categories in traditional and contemporary clogging styles (Jeff Driggs, email to author, May 18, 2011).

Club Culture and Conflicts

The MWSD movement incorporates several dance forms, but most participants look forward to the unpredictable, ever-moving, four-couple dances. MWSD dancers and callers generally agree that their activity attracts a large number of people educated in math, science, engineering, andinformation technology. Many people say that MWSD attracts these professions because MWSD itself is mathematical; the dance form is more about solving a puzzle than about technical proficiency. Another perspective is that people who work with computers all day naturally crave human social interaction. MWSD fills this need in safe, sober, welcoming environments where club members wear name badges, treat each other as friends, and hold hands and hug. MWSD dancers even have their own word for hug: Yellowrock (Rick Gittelman, interview by author, January 9, 2009; Mayo 2003, 77).

From the very beginning, MWSD club culture was about having fun and creating solidarity. When a club went to a festival or convention where other dancers were present, the club members brought matching club costumes to wear in the Grand March, a processional dance that concluded in a large auditorium where everyone danced together. At regular club danced, married couples often wore matching outfits. The men usually wore slacks or jeans, a bolo tie, a towel on their belt to wipe off sweat, and a button-down shirt with a yoke collar, long sleeves, and snap cuffs. It was commonly said that men wore sleeves because women did not want to touch their sweaty arms. The women often wore a dress (or blouse and skirt) with a high, unrevealing neck line. Underneath the skirt, they wore lacy pettipants or bloomers. A crinoline made the skirt fluff up, sometimes wider than a doorway. Some dancers (women) sewed their own attire, whereas others purchased their attire from MWSD apparel companies (Bob Brundage, interview by author, March 2, 2009).

Many dancers collected special badges to commemorate their MWSD accomplishments. Often, they punched holes in the special badges and dangled them from their club name badges, so the special badges became known as dangles. In 1959, Ray Lang invented the first special badge, the Knothead badge, after dancers from his Seattle, Washington club drove to Vancouver, British Columbia for a dance. The group concluded that they must have been knotheads to make such a trip, and Lang designed a badge for them: a piece of wood with a string passing through it. The Knothead badge caught on nationwide; it required four couples from a club to travel together at least 100 miles to attend a dance. Later, dancers who traveled more than 1,000 miles for a dance ordered Rover badges made out of sterling silver. Soon, there were badges or dangles for collecting 100 caller autographs, waking a caller up in the middle of the night to call a dance (and then serving him or her breakfast), dancing in a pool or a bathroom, and so on. At conventions, dancers did a Fun Badge tour and received a dangle for dancing at different local attractions (Mayo 2003, 79–80; Dennis Farrar, Betty Vaile, and Ted Vaile, interview by author, June 20, 2009).

In the 20th century, MWSD clubs were fairly homogenous; people recruited their friends, who were like themselves (Mayo 2003, 77). Frequently, married dancers wanted to dance with married people, and they did not want to change partners after each tip. Wives feared that if their husbands danced with another woman, especially an unwed woman, their husbands would be tempted to cheat on them. Husbands felt the same way about their wives dancing with other men. Some clubs were so strict about MWSD being a married couples' activity that even a long-time dancer who became single, whether through divorce or death of a spouse, could be voted out of the club. Gay dancers, who wanted to dance with someone of the same sex, often were ostracized. Some clubs went as far as meeting in private locations, to dodge laws about excluding people on the basis of race, ethnicity, or sexual orientation. All-African American MWSD and gay MWSD clubs developed as a result (Allan Hurst, e-mail to author, November 12, 2010).

The gay MWSD movement took off in the 1980s, and not only gay people joined the clubs. Many unwed, white, heterosexual people crossed over to gay MWSD. On average, the dancers were younger. Furthermore, the dancers changed partners after every tip Also, the

The Fun Badge Tour, dancing near the Washington Monument, at the 2009 International Association of Gay Square Dance Clubs Convention in Washington, D.C. Courtesy of Silke Heunisch.

dances were more energetic with extra details such as claps, spins, and kicks known as flourishes. And quite importantly, the gay MWSD clubs did not enforce a dress code. They dancers usually came in T-shirts, jeans, and sneakers. Caller Stephen Cole reflected on calling for gay MWSD groups, "They're younger, they move faster, and they make you work harder. In any one moment, a man may be dancing as a man or may be dancing as a woman. You have to pay attention" (interview by author, January 16, 2009).

The gay MWSD movement grew to include hundreds of clubs, including clubs in Canada, Mexico, and Japan, organized under the International Association of Gay Square Dance Clubs (IAGSDC). The Gay Callers Association (GCA) hosts an annual GCA Caller School to train callers who want to work with gay MWSD clubs. The All Join Hands Foundation is a non-profit organization that promotes gay MWSD and encourages new callers by offering scholarships to the GCA Caller School. Aside from the International Gay Square Dance Convention, gay MWSD clubs also organize weekend events called fly-ins. Gay MWSD do many of the same activities as straight MWSD clubs, but gay MWSD culture is more liberal about sexual innuendos, nudity, cross-dressing, and alcohol (after a dance). The Moonshine tip, or MWSD without clothing, represents this liberalism at its extreme. Not everyone participates in the Moonshine tip, which sometimes happens at special events such as fly-ins, but those who do could get a Moonshine dangle (Seth Levine and Gene Lauze, interview by author, December 18, 2008; David Anderson, interview by author, January 17, 2009).

When MWSD membership started to decline in the 1980s, the older straight dancers became more willing to dance with gay dancers. Barb Klein, who danceed with both types of MWSD clubs, explained how this shift came about,

> When the gay group first started trying to dance with the straight groups, particularly men were a little uncomfortable with two men dancing together . . . which is funny because men touch men in straight groups too, because that's what the calls do. When they start realizing that—first of all, that the gay guys or women are just regular people; and often they're the better dancers—not always, but lots of times they're really strong dancers—it became very desired to have them, because you need enough dancers to make squares. You want enough people. (interview by author, January 10, 2009)

The long-term success of the MWSD movement requires that different types of clubs collaborate and attend each others' events.

Increasingly, straight dancers and gay dancers are mixing, straight callers are calling for the community, and gay callers are calling for the straight community. Some National Square Dance Conventions feature a Rainbow Room, where gay dancers can be "bidansual," or dance in any position within the set, and add flourishes to the standard MWSD calls. At the 2009 convention in Long Beach, California, the author observed several teenagers leave the under-18 Youth Room and eagerly join in the Rainbow Room activities. The youngest dancers also joined gay dancers, often in all-male sets, in the Mainstream and Plus halls. The same year, a square of gay dancers and friends also won the very first dance competition at a national square dance convention, perhaps in part because they were more familiar with both gender roles, and they had better teamwork.

In the 21st century, most MWSD clubs have relaxed their dress code, realizing that some dancers cannot afford the expensive attire or are deterred by the look. Furthermore, young people in the 21st century do not want to take months of lessons before they can set foot in a MWSD club. In 2003, representatives from several organizations related to the MWSD movement met to form the Alliance of Round, Traditional and Square-Dance (ARTS), to promote their dance forms and attract new dancers, especially young people. In 2005, CALLERLAB adopted the Program Policy Initiative, encouraging experimentation with how to introduce the public to MWSD. Caller Rick Gittelman held afternoon Mainstream crash courses that covered as many calls as possible (Rick Gittelman, interview by author, January 9, 2009). The Wilde Bunch club in Albuquerque, New Mexico, offered a four-week program for beginners (Kris Jensen, interview, March 2, 2009). MWSD culture continues to evolve and innovate.

A National Folk Dance?

Is Square Dance the national folk dance of the United States? MWSD dancers often say yes. Traditional Square Dance enthusiasts generally say no. The question has caused a great deal of tension between dance communities. In the early 1980s, the newly formed United Square Dancers of America (USDA) lobbied U.S. Congress to have Square Dance declared the national folk dance. President Ronald Reagan approved the bill for 1982–1983, and Congress agreed to make the bill permanent if at least two-thirds of states accepted Square Dance a state dance, state folk dance, or state American folk dance. The first problem was that a state dance, like a state bird or a state flower, should be unique to that state. The bigger problem was that the bill appeared to represent a specific style of dancing and a type of people. Many Traditional Square Dance advocates believed that the USDA (made up of MWSD dancers) elevated MWSD, Round Dance, and their own style of Contra Dance above simpler, more repetitive rural dance forms. Furthermore, the bill largely overlooked the rich traditions of non-European groups who also contributed to American dance culture (Stan Fowler, interview by author, August 20, 2009).

There may never be an agreement about whether Square Dance is the national folk dance, or whether Square Dance is even a folk

8

Contra Dance

Contra Dance is another name for New England Square Dance, caller-led rural dances that mainly evolved from English and Scottish dances. Originally, the label *Contra Dance* encompassed square dances similar to European Quadrilles, circle dances, and longways dances (parallel lines). But since the mid-1970s, the term mainly has referred to longways dances. Similar to the rural Visiting Couple dances of the West, rural Contra Dance had about 20 simple figures and did not require lessons. Contra Dance callers had different styles of calling, but the dances were so repetitive that callers could stop calling during the dance, because the dancers had memorized the sequence. The sequence repeated over and over for seven or eight minutes, and couples stayed together but also danced with everyone in the set. Most sets contained no more than eight couples, and dancers typically changed partners after every dance (Bob Dalsemer, interview by author, August 19, 2009).

Before the 20th century, most New England longways dances were triple minor, so the dancers within a set grouped themselves into three-couple subsets. Partners stood across from each other, the women to the right of their partners when facing the caller/fiddler. Furthermore, these longways were proper, meaning that the women stood in one line and the men stood in another line (improper triple minor dances would have entailed the first couple crossing over, changing positions with one another). The first couple in each subset was the active couple; they did the figure while interacting with the second and third couple, who were considered semi-active or inactive. The inactive couples had more time to watch the active couple and to enjoy an unchaperoned conversation with their partners. At the end of one round of the dance, the actives moved down one place, away from the caller, to dance with two new inactive couples from the next set. This meant that the original third couples became second couples the next time through, third couples the third time through, and so on, as they moved toward the caller. For all triple minor dances, when any couple reached the end of the entire set, they had to wait out two rounds of the dance before reentering the set from the opposite direction. Duple minor dances for two-couple subsets began to replace triple minor dances in the early 20th century, because two-couple subsets permitted more dancing time. When a couple reached the end of the set, they only had to wait out one sequence. For any improper dance, when a couple reached the end of the set, they had to switch sides with their partner before reentering (Holden 1956, 2–5; Walkowitz 2010, 44; David Millstone, interview by author, August 19, 2009).

By the late 19th century, contra music had a distinct sound, created by French Canadians, Cape Breton Scots, and Irish immigrants who settled in mill towns together and shared their tunes and instruments (Walkowitz 2010, 46). The main instrument was a fiddle, usually played by the caller. Most tunes consisted of four eight-measure parts, following the pattern AABB. Each dance sequence had four parts, corresponding to the musical structure. Some dance venues added a piano or organ in the early 20th century, but the fiddle still carried the tune (Holden 1956, 8–9). Dances such as Money Musk, Hull's Victory, Chorus Jig, Petronella, Girl I Left Behind Me, Rory O'More, and Pop

Contra Dance variations, adapted from dance formations in Playford's *The English Dancing-Master* (1651). Author's archives.

Dancers at the 2009 Albuquerque Folk Festival with caller William "Doc" Litchman (far right) at the head of the set. These dancers are in proper formation, with the men in the left line and the women in the right line, partners standing across from one another. Before the dance starts, the dancers grab hands in duple minor subsets to determine their direction of travel (progression) as couples. Author's archives.

Goes the Weasel were tied to a specific tune (Holden 1956, 9). Other dances were done to any tune with the correct tempo, quality, and phrasing.

Ralph Page

The recreational Square Dance revival in the 1940s drew attention to Contra Dance, but only temporarily. In the 1950s, many New England callers turned their attention to the Modern Square Dance movement. Ralph Page was one of the only callers to promote Contra Dance in the 1950s and 1960s, until Contra Dance was absorbed by the counterculture movement and evolved into a nationwide activity. From 1943 to 1968, Page took a train each week to call at the Boston, Massachusetts, YWCA, and he also called in small towns. He promoted a smooth and elegant style of dancing. Contra Dance enthusiasts celebrate Ralph Page for keeping the old dances alive, and every year the New England Folk Festival Association (NEFFA) hosts a Ralph Page Dance

Legacy Weekend in his honor (Millstone 2007; New England Folk Festival Association, n.d.).

Page began calling dances in Keene, New Hampshire in 1930. From 1935 to 1937, he wrote a series of articles for the magazine *Yankee* in Dublin, New Hampshire. Page collaborated with Beth Tolman, a staff member at *Yankee*, to publish *The Country Dance Book* in 1937. It was the first significant book about New England Contra Dance since Burchenal's *American Country-Dances* in 1918 (Holden 1956, 9–10). Page called at the 1939–1940 World's Fair in New York City, the same fair that launched Michael Herman's career teaching RIFD. After Page served as master of ceremonies for the first New England Folk Dance Festival in 1944, he cofounded the New England Folk Festival Association in 1945 (Casey 1981, 29). Musician Bob McQuillen, who got his start accompanying Ralph Page in 1947, called Page "the most famous Contra Dance caller in the world at the time" (Bob McQuillen, interview by author, July 12, 2009).

During the McCarthy era, when the Modern Square Dance movement and International Folk Dance movement diverged, Page, who specialized in Traditional Square Dance, continued to interact with the RIFD community. He called at major RIFD camps, including the Hermans' Maine Camp and Lawton Harris's Folk Dance Camp in Stockton, California. He started his own folk dance camp in New Hampshire in 1950, at which Michael and Mary Ann Herman were guest teachers. In 1956, Page was one of five American folk dance leaders who went on the Japan tour organized by Earl Buckley. In 1966, the English Folk Song and Dance Society sponsored Page on a tour to England. Page also produced numerous records (some on Herman's Folk Dancer label) and published the *Northern Junket* magazine (1949–1984) (Bob Dalsemer, interview, August 19, 2009; Casey 1981, 29–30).

The Folk Music Revival and Back to the Land

In 1928, poet and biographer Carl Sandburg published *The American Songbag*, which gave credence to the idea that a valuable American rural music tradition existed. The Library of Congress inaugurated its Archive of the American Folk-Song two years later. Several musicologists collected "roots" music across the nation in the 1930s. After World War II, record companies recognized the potential for roots records, including race records with African American music, as well as old-time records with acoustic string bands. In the late 1950s, roots music was absorbed into a folk music revival focused on civil rights and peace. In 1964, Dave Freeman started Country Records, the first record label dedicated to old-time music (Bealle 2005, 3, 17–18; Walkowitz 2010, 165).

In the 1960s, the Newport Folk Festival in Rhode Island helped transform the folk music revival into a boom, and it also exposed many people to folk dance. The Country Dance Society presented exhibitions at the first festival in 1959 and (renamed as the Country Dance and Song Society) in 1967. The early Newport Folk Festivals placed dance exhibitions between music performances, but the 1967 festival offered day-long participatory workshops on Contra Dance, Balkan Dance, Square Dance, Lancers and Quadrilles, International Dance, and English Country Dance. Page and Margot Mayo led the American Square Dance and Contra Dance. The Hermans and Cornell (Conny) and Marianne Taylor, RIFD leaders in Boston, led the International and Balkan sessions. May Gadd and Art Cornelius, a CDSS leader in Boston, directed a mixed American and English folk dance program (Walkowitz 2010, 200).

By 1967, the folk music revival had lost some of its political vigor. Two years earlier, Bob Dylan had plugged in his guitar at the Newport Folk Festival, transforming his characteristic natural sound into a style that resonated more with the rock 'n' roll audience. Many folkies turned away from acoustic folk music and toward new folk-rock rhythms, celebrating the beat more than the lyrics. As the Vietnam War escalated, however, a mass social and cultural movement united hippies and social activists, and both groups embraced traditional folk music and folk dance as part of their mission. Many college students, fed up with commercialism, materialism, and waste, moved to New England to go back to the land (Walkowitz 2010, 200–202; Bealle 2005, 3).

The back to the landers romanticized rural life. They perceived traditional culture as a viable alternative to negative effects of modernism such as wasteful consumerism, racism, social alienation, and environmental degradation. Many of these people wore bell-bottoms and Birkenstock sandals. Haircuts, shaving, and underwear were not popular. They lived on communes with likeminded people, used oil lamps instead of electricity, cut their own firewood, grew their own food, and handcrafted musical instruments and household items (Millstone 2007; Steve Hickman, interview, August 19, 2009).

Dudley Laufman was an early back to the lander who latched onto Contra Dance. Laufman grew up in a Boston suburb and encountered rural music and dance while working on a dairy farm in Fremont, New Hampshire. In the late 1940s, Laufman attended the New England Folk Festival, where he heard McQuillen playing accordion with several fiddlers. Afterward, Laufman decided to attend Page's dances in Boston. He moved to Canterbury, New Hampshire in 1959 and built a cabin with a dirt floor, and he lived hand to mouth with odd jobs. He called dances, played harmonica and accordion, published poetry, and organized musicians for busking. When back to the landers flocked to rural Vermont and New Hampshire in the 1960s, they discovered Dudley dances through word of mouth, and they could relate to Laufman because he was like them (Nevell 1977, 100; Bealle 2005, 39; Millstone 2007).

Laufman revitalized community dances in rural New England with an influx of energetic young people who followed him. He called at several places, including town halls, dance camps, folk festivals, and college campuses. Back to the landers and college students, many of them RIFD enthusiasts, were known to drive for hours, hitchhike across states, and pitch tents in fields in order to attend a Dudley dance. Laufman called a variety of dance formations, and he popularized a vigorous, rustic style of dancing with improvised Clogging. The back to the landers caught on immediately. They easily imagined rural townspeople from a century or two earlier dancing the same dances, in the same style, in the same town halls. Culture clashes sometimes happened on the dance floor when truckloads of young people who danced Laufman's style in bare feet converged with townspeople who dressed in their best clothing and used a more elegant, upright style (David Millstone, interview by author, August 19, 2009; Walkowitz 2010, 210).

In the 1960s, Laufman began a loosely organized orchestra called the Canterbury Country Dance Orchestra (CCDO). The CCDO played at the Newport Folk Festival in 1965 and introduced thousands of people to Contra Dance. In 1966, the CCDO was the official band for the first Fox Hollow Festival, in Petersburgh, New York. In the 1970s, the group produced a series of records that had liner notes depicting Contra Dance as deeply rooted in rural life (Bealle 2005, 39). By this time, CCDO was the band of choice for socialite weddings in Boston and the top Contra Dance band in the country. Aspiring Contra Dance musicians looked to them for inspiration. In 1974, the group popularized Contra Dance in Washington, D.C., through the National Folk Festival (Millstone 2007). Prior to their appearance, only a few dancers in the Baltimore area did Contra Dance as taught by Joe Blundon, a former Harvard Law School student who had danced with Page in Boston (Bob Dalsemer, interview by author, August 19, 2009).

As the Contra Dance movement gained momentum, Dudley's followers demanded more dances than the caller could provide by himself. Several new callers, including Fred Breunig, Jerry Jenkins, Cammy Kaynor, Chris Madigan, Jack Perron, and Tod Whittemore, stepped up to call weekly dances. In the early 1970s, James (Jim) Morrison and John Wheeler also started an English and American dance at Lynchburg College, in Lynchburg, Virginia (John Wheeler, interview by David Millstone, August 20, 2009). Many Contra Dance enthusiasts began to attend CDSS events, especially Pinewoods Camp, to satisfy their dance craving. CDSS started another camp at Buffalo Gap in West Virginia, because Pinewoods could not accommodate all the people who wanted to attend.

The Contra Dance followers, many of them from International Folk Dance, shifted the type of people who attended of CDSS events, bringing more people of non-Anglo heritage (especially Jews and Italians) onto the dance floor (Walkowitz 2010, 209). Their growing presence at CDSS events, loose dance style, and liberal behavior often raised concern among older, more conservative CDSS members. Pinewoods campers from the 1970s affectionately recall how May Gadd patrolled at night with her torch (flashlight) in search of indecent activity in the bushes.

Changes in Choreography and CDSS

Changes to Contra Dance choreography happened slowly at first. In the 1950s and 1960s, Ralph Page almost singlehandedly kept the New England rural dances alive, and he preserved the dances as he had learned them (Mayo 2003, 9). In the 1950s, Modern Western Square Dance caller Herbie Gaudreau introduced a couple-facing-couple longways formation, where partners rotated 90 degrees and stood side by side in the same line. In the 1970s, this formation became known as the Becket formation, named after the YMCA camp in

Becket, Massachusetts where Gaudreau taught. Over a 20-year period, Gaudreau wrote over 100 longways dances that were all-moving;
everyone played an active role until they reached the end of the set,
and then they waited out one sequence. These dances mainly were
done in at MWSD venues; they not popular among folk revivalists
most likely because they lacked a partner swing (Parkes 1996).

Several non-MWSD Contra Dance callers wrote all-moving longways dances in the 1970s and 1980s, and these dances gradually replaced
the traditional dances. Contra Dance enthusiasts labeled the older
dances Chestnuts, inspired by musicians Rodney and Randy Miller
who produced two albums titled *New England Chestnuts* (Smukler and
Millstone 2008, 7–8). The new dances introduced new traveling patterns
and new figures, such as the Gypsy figure from English Country Dance
(introduced by Ted Sannella). For the Gypsy, two dancers stared in
each other's eyes while walking in a circle, and oftentimes the Gypsy
melted into a Swing. For the Swing, a couple stood right shoulder to
right shoulder in closed dance position (although there were variations on the embrace) and locked eyes while spinning in a circle. They
either used a bouncing walk or a buzz step, keeping the right foot
almost planted while pushing off the left foot in a skateboarding motion. The dancers gained momentum by giving weight, leaning back
slightly into each other's arms. Over time, the swing increased from
eight counts to 16 counts, and dancers sometimes complained if a
program did not have enough swinging (David Millstone, interview
by author, August 19, 2009).

Boston area callers Tony Parkes and Ted Sannella wrote some of the
earliest all-moving dances for the New England Contra Dance community in the 1970s. Parkes, originally from New York City, started
calling dances at the Farm and Wilderness Camps in Vermont in 1964.
His first dance compositions were Shadrack's Delight (1972) and Infla-
tion Reel (1973). Parkes moved to Boston in 1973 to be closer to the heart
of the Contra Dance revival. Sannella, from the Boston area, became a
professional caller in 1946. He called English Country Dance as well
as Contra Dance, and he composed a series of three-couple dances
using ECD figures and structure. These dances became known as Ted's
Triplets. In 1982, Sannella published *Balance and Swing*, a collection of
55 New England dances. Larry Jenning's *Zesty Contras* (1983) and Gene
Hubert's three volumes of *Dizzy Dances*, published by 1986, focused specifically on all-moving longways dances.

The 1973 CDSS Pinewoods Camp in was different than previous years. Before, the camp had hired American dance teachers, mainly from the John C. Campbell Folk School, Berea College, and the Pine Mountain Settlement (Bealle 2005, 154). But at the 1973 camp, Sannella called Contra Dance one week, Laufman called Contra Dance the next week, and Morrison called southern Appalachian Square Dance the third week. Pinewoods and CDSS in general were shifting toward a more equal representation of English dance and American dance. The first generation of Cecil Sharp-influenced CDSS leaders were graying or gone, and May Gadd had retired from her 45-year term as national director in 1972. Genevieve (Genny) Shimer temporarily filled Gadd's former position for one year, and then Jim Morrison took over as national director. Morrison, fresh out of Dartmouth College, had interned at the John C. Campbell Folk School, organized a Dudley dance at Dartmouth, and was part of the Contra Dance revival movement (Walkowitz 2010, 214–215).

Many changes happened to CDSS after Gadd's retirement. In 1973, the council that ran CDS activities in New York reorganized as the New York Dance Activities Committee (NYDAC) to allow for greater membership across dance communities. Furthermore, in 1974, ECD enthusiast Patrick Noel Shuldham-Shaw (known as Pat Shaw), from England, came to Pinewoods for the first time. Many traditionalists, who believed in the authenticity of Sharp's interpretations of the Playford dances, had blacklisted Shaw because he composed original English Country Dances based on the Playford structure and style. Shaw composed his first dance, "Monica's Delight," at age 13 in 1930. He went on to create approximately 171 original dances, sometimes borrowing American dance figures and he encouraged other ECD enthusiasts to do the same. He also revised figures in Playford dances that he believed Sharp misinterpreted from the 17th century *Dancing Master* series. Shaw suggested that the contemporary people who did the dances were the folk, and that the origins of the dances did not matter. His arrival at Pinewoods in 1974 launched a Modern English Country Dance (MECD) movement.

By the mid-1970s, live music had become the new standard at English Country Dance events, inspired by the folk music revival and Contra Dance movement. This meant that a caller (not a record) determined the length of a dance. The most influential ECD band, based on output, was Bare Necessities, made up of Jacqueline Schwab (piano), Peter

Barnes (flute and whistles), Earl Gaddis (violin), and Mary Lea (viola). By 2008, Bare Necessities had recorded 177 tunes on 12 CDs. They played the tunes at about 104 beats per minute, about 25 percent slower than ECD from Sharp's era. The tunes often were in triple meter, supporting a flowing, balletic quality that was easy on aging dancers' knees. Aspiring ECD musicians learned tunes by listening to the Bare Necessities' CDs. Later, they learned the tunes directly from Barnes's two volumes of *The Barnes Book of English Country Dance Tunes* (1986 and 2006), known as *Barnes* in the ECD community, which collectively contain almost 900 tunes (Walkowitz 2010, 246–247).

CDSS became more liberal in the 1970s with new English choreography and a broader scope of participants. With Morrison as national director, the society also began to promote more Morris Dance and Sword Dance. A few Morris Dance sides (teams) and Sword Dance teams existed in the United States before 1973. In 1963, Nibs Matthews, a Morris Dance leader in England, taught at Pinewoods Camp and encouraged campers to form the Pinewoods Morris Men. The club formed in 1964, and Gadd supported the dancers because of their affiliation with the camp (she perceived English dance groups outside of CDSS as a threat). Pinewoods Camp became a training ground for American Morris Dance leaders in the 1970s, resulting in the Binghamton Morris Men, Cambridge Morris Men, Greenwich Morris Men, and the first American all-female side, Ring O'Bells. Many Morris Dance sides organized as clubs and joined the Morris Ring federation (founded in London in 1934). Morris Dance events and competitions introduced many dancers to English Sword Dance, both rapper (flexible sword) and longsword (Graetz 1989; Walkowitz 2010, 153, 224).

In 1983, Brad Foster, Morris Dance enthusiast who received the first Pinewoods Morris Men scholarship in 1975, became the national director of CDSS. The same year, Bob Dalsemer published *West Virginia Square Dances*, with a forward by Jim Morrison, a collection of rural dances based on Dalsemer's fieldwork in West Virginia in 1977–1978. Dalsemer's work enriched CDSS activities with American dances that had not been recorded previously. Also in the 1980s, CDSS leaders made a bold move that blatantly contrasted with the society's Anglo reputation; they brought a Break Dance team to Pinewoods. David Shewmaker, former chef at Pinewoods, remembered, "[The break dancers] were great. All the kids were in love with those guys. I think they were hired for diversity" (interview by author, August 22, 2009).

In 1987, CDSS headquarters moved from New York to Northampton, Massachusetts. The move forced NYDAC to reorganize as Country Dance * New York (CD * NY), an autonomous chapter of CDSS. In 1989, the headquarters relocated to Haydenville, Massachusetts. The move meant that CDSS activities were no longer centered in New York, and the rural site helped CDSS represent itself as national. By this time, the society had several Canadian members, so the title of national director changed to executive and artistic director (Walkowitz 2010, 215, 236).

A Nationwide Contra Dance Movement

Living off the land proved more difficult than many back to the landers expected. Some of these people left New England and started regularly scheduled Contra Dance events dances in places that had never experienced these dances. Furthermore, a growing number of teens and young adults were applying for colleges and graduate schools farther from home. Young adults who had been raised in New England brought their music and dance knowledge to college campuses across the nation. Also, young people who lived outside of New England and were affiliated with the CDSS community commonly went to Pinewoods or other CDSS camps and discovered Contra Dance (Walkowitz 2010, 227, Bealle 2005, 152).

Innovative and experimental Contra Dance bands in the 1970s and 1980s also helped spread Contra Dance. Some of the most famous bands from this era were Swallowtail, Wild Asparagus, Yankee Ingenuity, and various ensembles organized by David Kaynor. David Cantieni, who cofounded Swallowtail in 1978 and Wild Asparagus in 1984, reflected about the bands, "People tried all kinds of tunes: Beatles tunes, old Swing tunes, show tunes. Anything that's 32 bars and [had] the right phrasing [was] fair game" (interview by author, August 20, 2009). Wild Asparagus was one of the most widely traveled bands in the early 1980s. George Marshall was the caller, there was no fiddle, and the band became known for their wild improvisations on concertina, oboe, and piano (Bealle 2005, 252–253).

Dudley Laufman fell into the background of the Contra Dance movement by the 1980s. David Millstone, who produced the documentary *The Other Way Back* (2007) about Laufman, explained, "[Dudley] couldn't compete in the emerging complex Contra Dance scene

Contra Dance at the 2009 Ghost Town Chill Down, in Jerome, Arizona. Author's archives.

and didn't want to" (interview by author, August 19, 2009). Laufman picked up a fiddle and focused his efforts on the youngest members of society through school programs and family dances. He rejected the contemporary music and choreography and returned to the very traditional sounds and dances (Millstone 2007).

Contra Dance groups used records when musicians were not available, but records lost favor to live Contra Dance bands in the 1980s. Live bands brought excitement to the dance by changing the tune, meter, or key. They added or omitted instruments to change the sound. They played off the dancers' energy, and the dancers felt viscerally connected to the moment. Through good music and repetitive movement, dancers often experienced a trancelike state. Some people traveled long distances to dance to certain bands and callers, and the ones who traveled often for dances affectionately called themselves dance gypsies.

Dances became longer in the 1980s when bands introduced medleys, playing several tunes back to back in the same song. Instead of seven or eight minutes, dances lasted 10 to 15 minutes. The sets also became longer to accommodate more dancers at an evening dance event. The callers no longer had enough time to teach English Country Dance, International Folk Dance, ballroom dance and other dance forms that had been popular at New England community dance events in the 1970s. Other dance forms gradually were filtered out, although some dances featured a sound-check Polka or Waltz while the musicians were setting up, and most dances kept a Waltz before an intermission and a Waltz as the last dance. Starting in Boston, in the mid-1970s, Contra Dance enthusiasts began to use the term "contra dance" for a dance event that predominantly featured longways sets (David Millstone, interview by author, August 19, 2009; Bob Dalsemer, interview by author, August 19, 2009).

Societies and centers and with the words "old-time," "folk," "folklore," and "country" in their names sprouted up across the country mostly during the folk music revival years and into the early 1980s. Some examples were the Folklore Society of Greater Washington (1964), the Folk Arts Center of New England (1975), and the Bay Area Country Dance Society (1980). Many of these groups promoted contra dances when the activity spread nationwide in the 1970s and 1980s. They collected and produced resources to keep dancers informed about regional dance activities. They hosted singer/songwriting workshops, house parties that featured acoustic bands, and myriad folk dance activities, including American rural dance forms Balkan Dance, Cajun Dance, English Country Dance, family dances, International Folk Dance, Israeli Dance, play-party games, Playford balls, Scottish Country Dance, and Vintage Dance (Linda and Ron Nieman, interview by author, May 16, 2009).

The proximity of cities and abundance of contra dances along the East Coast sustained a large pool of callers and musicians. In the Boston area, for example, it was possible to attend a contra dance just about every night of the week. Outside of New England, Contra Dance leaders often hired New England callers and bands to call at regularly scheduled dances and dance weekends. The high-energy New England bands began to influence musicians in other parts of the country. In southern Appalachia, for example, Contra Dance originally was done to southern Appalachian style music until the New England bands started touring and selling CDs the 1980s (Bob Dalsemer, interview by author, August 19, 2009).

Carl Wittman pioneered a gender-free (sometimes gender-role free or gender neutral) dance movement that gained several followers in the 1980s. Wittman, a certified Royal Scottish Country Dance Society instructor, taught Scottish Country Dance in the San Francisco area around 1970. He felt stifled by the traditional gender roles in English and Scottish dance, and he officially came out as gay in 1969. In 1971, Wittman moved to a gay commune in Wolf Creek, Oregon, where he became involved with Alan Troxler. Wittman and Troxler sought to modify country dances in a way that did not enforce traditional gender roles. They used green and red "pinnies" of cloth or paper, so that dancers were able to recognize each other's positions by color instead of gender. They also used gender-neutral language, which they believed would create a more inclusive environment. Their community dances attracted families, gay men, lesbians, and friends (Walkowitz 2010, 233; Ricciotti 2006, 37).

The gender-free dance movement spread nationwide from the 1970s through the 1980s, but it did not gain the same momentum as the gay MWSD movement. In part, this was because preexisting Contra Dance groups generally were more welcoming of people with alternative lifestyles, because the dancers themselves often dodged mainstream culture. In Jamaica Plain (Boston), Massachusetts, Michael Ciccone founded a gender-free English Country Dance group, and Chris Ricciotti started a gender-free Contra Dance and Square Dance group. In 1988, the gay and lesbian folk dance groups in the Boston area federated as the Lavender Folk and Country Dancers. By 2006, gender-free Contra Dance communities existed in Massachusetts, New York, Michigan, Minnesota, and California. Furthermore, gender-free or gay International Folk Dance groups practiced in Jamaica Plain, Brattleboro, Vermont and San Francisco, California. Gender-free or gay Scottish and/or English dance groups also existed in North Carolina and Oregon (Walkowitz 2010, 234; Ricciotti 2006, 42–43).

By the early 21st century, each region of the United States had a distinct Contra Dance culture. For example, near Washington, D.C., the contra dances at Glen Echo Park, a former amusement park preserved by the National Park Service, attracted hundreds of dancers and dozens of musicians on open band nights. The Boston area dances were energetic, and the men sometimes wore skirts or kilts to keep cool. The dances in Asheville, North Carolina and Greenfield, Massachusetts were known for their strong youth presence. The Nelson, New Hampshire Monday Night dance was over 100 years old, which gave dancers and musicians a sense of connecting to the past. The town hall's slanted floor only added to its historic character. The dances in Santa Cruz, California had a mix of businesspeople and young social activists and environmentalists, and some of these young people traveled by freight train to folk festivals on the East Coast. Dances in each region were influenced by the atmosphere of the venues as well as the types of people who lived there (Ethan Hazzard-Watkins, interview by author, August 18, 2009).

Ethan Hazzard-Watkins, a Contra Dance musician in Brattleboro, Vermont, who served as the CDSS Youth Projects Intern from 2008 to 2009, described the new generation of musicians and dancers that participate in the Contra Dance movement,

> The scene that I'm really a part of, and that I connected to, is very creative, very accepting of innovation. . . . Where I live, there's a really strong local organic food movement—people who are farmers, people who are home gardeners, people who are food activists of one kind or another. I think that this group has a strong natural affinity for contra dancing. . . . [Some dancers] are connected to this sort of punk, activist, old-time-music, organic-food, dumpster-diving, hopping-freight-trains kind of scene. (interview by author, August 18, 2009)

The young adult crew at the 2009 CDSS Timber Ridge Camp (formerly the Buffalo Gap CDSS Camp) agreed that the new generation of dancers were interested in social activism and environmentalism. Many of them volunteered in their communities, college campuses, and even overseas (focus group with author, August 20, 2009).

Elvie Miller, a musician and weaver, and daughter of musician Rodney Miller, became involved in the Contra Dance community as a child by going to regular dances and dance camps such as Pinewoods Family Week. She describes what a contra dance was like for her as a child and how the community treated her,

> My brother and I would just play by ourselves. We took sleeping bags and set them up in back of the stage and went to sleep at some point during the dance. That was a big part of our growing up. . . . The other thing that I look back and see now is it was such a strong community, and there were so many adults who were interested in me as a kid and just wanting to include me. I was definitely dancing at a very young age because the adults were so welcoming and inclusive. (interview by author, August 20, 2009)

In high school, Miller joined her father in playing music for dances. After college, she received a Watson Fellowship to study traditional

Dancers at the 2009 CDSS combined English and American Week/Family Week at Timber Ridge Camp in West Virginia do a Waltz during an evening dance. Author's archives.

music and dance in Europe. Miller moved to Ireland, where she continues to play music, but she still participates in contra dances when she comes to the United States to visit. For many young people who grow up in the contra dance community, the music and dancing becomes a core part of their identity.

As Miller's story illustrates, the integration of different generations at the dance event is essential for the continuation of the Contra Dance movement. Today, there are many CDSS activities and other Contra Dance events directed toward youth, including Berea College's Christmas Country Dance School, the Youth Dance Weekend, family dances, and family dance camps. Weeklong events usually include a variety of dances, games, songs, parties, and responsibilities such as sweeping floors or washing dishes. Children and teens make friends and learn new skills, but they also learn what it means to be part of a larger community. The CDSS New Leaders, Good Leaders Fund has contributed greatly to the Contra Dance movement, and the folk dance movement in general, by awarding scholarships to young dancers, sponsoring youth-dance events, and organizing caller workshops and leadership development initiatives so that a new generation will be able to sustain the educational, recreational, multifaceted folk dance movement.

Conclusion

The folk dance movement began in the 1890s, a time when American and European cities were industrializing and attracting new workers, resulting in class tensions and social anxieties. British and North American social reformers and educators believed that social conditions would improve by uplifting the poorest and most impressionable people through physical fitness, fresh air, and organized play. Gymnastics and gymnastics dancing paved the way for folk dancing as part of the social reform. At first, folk dancing was taught in settlement houses, playgrounds, and public schools. The majority of dances came from northwestern Europe, because these dances supposedly possessed qualities that would to promote health, social skills, and democratic attitudes. When African American dance forms became popular in the early 20th century, white moralists and folk dance educators advertised folk dancing as a more wholesome activity than going to dance halls.

In the United States, English folk dance leaders infused the folk dance movement with Morris Dance, Sword Dance, and English Country Dance in the 1910s. They planted the seeds for an American branch of the English Folk Dance Society, which later separated from its parent and evolved into the Country Dance and Song Society. English dance in the United States primarily attracted people who were of Anglo-Saxon Protestant heritage and financially secure. Folk dance leaders both in England and the United States believed that English dance would help society by reawakening the Anglo spirit they attributed to each nation. Musicologists, anthropologists, and folklorists began traveling into southern Appalachia to document songs and dances that were thought to be English, supposedly preserved in mountainous isolation for centuries. What they found instead were original American songs and dances, created when different cultural groups met and blended their traditions.

In the 1920s and 1930s, Americans began to accept that original American folk traditions existed. Previously, most Americans believed that their own rural music and dance forms were watered down versions of European traditions. At this time, the folk dance movement largely overlooked Native American and African American contributions to American dance culture. Schoolteachers and youth group leaders had minimal knowledge about real Native American dance forms. They mostly taught composed dances that depicted Native Americans as spiritual or savage, based on stereotypes perpetuated by popular media. Early Clogging and Tap Dance manuals represented African Americans as caricatures from blackface minstrelsy, suggesting that African Americans were uneducated, lazy, and childlike. Nineteenth century theories about race evolution supported the idea that northwestern Europeans were the most civilized, and most folk dance leaders could not see beyond European peasants and their North American equivalents as the folk. Rustic people of European origin supposedly were pure, simple, and in tune with nature.

The folk dance movement gained momentum during the Great Depression with WPA initiatives, folk festivals, rural retreats, and a shift toward adult group recreation and club activities. The 1939–1940 World's Fairs in New York City and San Francisco featured folk dance exhibition groups and introduced thousands of people to participatory folk dancing. Square Dance exhibition groups proved to city dwellers that American rural dance forms did not have to be rowdy and unrefined, as these dance forms so often were stereotyped. During World War II, folk dance enthusiasts promoted American Square Dance as a patriotic activity. The urban recreational folk dance movement gained a large adult following around Chicago, New York City, San Francisco. The California folk dance clubs created two federations and standardized the dances, so that dancers from different clubs could meet at a festival and dance together.

The growth of the record industry after World War II fueled the recreational folk dance movement by enabling clubs to form in areas that did not have live musicians. At this time, international dances and

American dances often happened in the same venue. The majority of RIFD repertoire consisted of northwestern European couple dances. These dances were similar to the old-time ballroom dances, such as the Polka and Waltz, done in between the square sets in recreational Square Dance clubs. In the 1950s, though, RSD enthusiasts turned their attention to Modern Square Dance. RIFD absorbed nonpartner Israeli dances and Kolos from former Yugoslavia, as well as foreign teachers, counterculture supporters, and communist sympathizers.

The Modern Square Dance and International Folk Dance communities diverged even more in the 1960s. Modern Square Dance evolved into Modern Western Square Dance, an activity that required dancers to take lessons before they could participate at a club. International Folk Dance enthusiasts became enamored of Balkan dances. Highly skilled state-sponsored national folk music and dance ensembles from the Soviet Union and Eastern Bloc encouraged RIFD dancers to learn professional choreography. Frequently, RIFD dancers did not realize that the dances were recent inventions. The ensembles also encouraged Americans to create their own International Folk Dance performance groups. In the 1970s, Balkan dance enthusiasts traveled to the Balkans, where they heard live music and realized that the dances they learned in RIFD clubs were not always congruent with how regular people in the Balkans actually danced. This disparity, along with the diminishing quality of RIFD recordings, influenced many folk dancers to leave the RIFD community and start separate Balkan music and dance community. Other RIFD-related folk dance groups followed, and RIFD dancers crossed over into other types of dance activities.

The post–World War II folk music revival heightened public interest in acoustic old-time music and encouraged many young Americans to pick up instruments and write songs for social change. These people attended folk festivals and folk music camps, and they organized societies dedicated to the preservation of old-time music and folk songs. The folk music revival lost momentum when rock 'n' roll became popular, but the escalation of the Vietnam War in the 1960s brought a new wave of conscientious objectors, war protesters, and hippies into the folk music revival. These people viewed traditional culture as a viable alternative to the problems produced by mainstream American culture. Many of them went to rural New England to live off the land.

In New England, the back to the landers encountered Contra Dance, a rural dance form that had almost died out in the early 20th century. Ralph Page almost singlehandedly kept the dance form alive in small towns and Boston. Dudley Laufman introduced the back to the landers and local college students to rural community dances. He popularized a grounded, improvisatory style of dancing, and his Canterbury Country Dance Orchestra inspired many young people to become Contra Dance musicians. Contra Dance enthusiasts filtered into CDSS dances and camps. They brought a liberal attitude and sexual energy that concerned English dance traditionalists. By the 1970s, though, the original CDSS leadership, put in place by Cecil Sharp, was aging or gone. The new generation leaders recognized that CDSS had to be more inclusive in order to survive. CDSS opened its doors to the counterculture, embraced new choreography for English Country Dance, and promoted American Square Dance, Morris Dance, and Sword Dance.

CDSS events sometimes include non-European dance and music forms for diversity, but not to overpower the society's original English emphasis. In *City Folk: English Country Dance and the Politics of Folk in Modern America*, Daniel Walkowitz concludes, "CDSS preserves a sanitized 'American' legacy without reference to dance of Native Americans, free blacks, the plantation, or the reservation. . . . The challenge for CDSS will be to incorporate dances with 'thrusting hips' as an integral part of the folk tradition within the Country Dance and Song Society of America" (Walkowitz 2010, 274). No doubt, the scope of the folk dance movement has grown, and the challenge is now which dances to select from a very large pool of possibilities.

The modern perception of a folk dance is any dance tied to a group of people, the folk. Folk dances may belong to an imaginary group of peasants. They may be brand new creations with a known choreographer. They may be African, Asian, European, Middle Eastern, Polynesian—from virtually anywhere. The International Folk Dance movement depended on immigrants and foreign travel for a constant supply of new dances, and RIFD dancers also reached out to Native Americans. The RIFD community's inherent desire to represent people from all parts of the world certainly helped promote the notion that all cultural groups had valuable folk dances. After World War II, American soldiers even brought back a dance from Japan, Tanko Bushi, the Japanese Coalmining Dance, which remains popular in RIFD clubs.

Several cultural shifts contributed to a more inclusive folk dance movement. In the 1940s, the theory of cultural relativism replaced outdated theories of race evolution that supported colonial initiatives by suggesting northwestern Europeans were the superior race. Cultural relativism suggested that all cultural groups were unique and evolved independently. World War II drew Americans' attention to the importance of cross-cultural understanding for international peace. The civil rights era of the 1950s and 1960s furthered the idea that all humans were equal, and that all cultural groups had valuable traditions to contribute. The Immigration and Nationality Act of 1965 replaced the Immigration Act of 1924, which strongly favored immigration from northwestern European nations. The number of first-generation immigrants living in the United States quadrupled from 1965 to 2007, reaching 38 million. Immigration from Asia, Mexico, and Latin America increased substantially.

Greater mobility also made the folk dance movement more inclusive, because people increasingly had to interact with others beyond their local community. The National Interstate and Defense Highways Act of 1956 facilitated cross-country travel. The Airline Deregulation Act of 1978 made air travel more affordable. By the 21st century, many Americans traveled long distances for college and moved regularly for work. Increased leisure travel, overseas work, foreign exchange programs for students, antidiscrimination laws, diversity quotas, community service, and social networking on the Internet ensured that Americans would come into contact with people of diverse backgrounds, from all parts of the world.

Increased mobility and enhanced communication, through the Internet and mobile phones with nationwide or international coverage, directly influenced the folk dance movement, as well. Folk dance travel always existed, as shown by Mary Wood Hinman and Elizabeth Burchenal's trips to Europe to collect folk dances and folk songs in the early 20th century. Balkan music and dance enthusiasts did the festival circuit in Eastern Europe starting in the 1970s. This inspired folk dance leaders to organize folk dance vacations and cruises in other places, including China, Russia, and Turkey. Ironically, the growth of folk dance camps, weekends, and vacations sometimes created a problem for regularly scheduled dances, because dancers stopped going to their local community dances and only went to the dance intensives.

People who complain about the decline of folk dancing usually participate in dance communities that are not well structured to support the needs and interests of young people in the 21st century. This does not mean folk dancing is dying out. The term "folk dancing," however, has become ambiguous. Since the 1890s, folk dancing has overlapped with peasant dances, ballroom dances, and professionally choreographed dances. To complicate the matter, popular dances often become folk dances when they are no longer popular. The Cakewalk of the 1900s could be a folk dance, as could the Macarena of the 1990s. Today, the term covers such a broad range that it is best to use more specific terminology for dance forms and dance communities. Many people perceive folk dancing as outdated or dying out, without seeing it as part of a greater social dance movement that is constantly adapting and bringing people together.

People who consider themselves part of social dance communities know the satisfaction and sense of purpose that can be achieved through the unparalleled experience of dancing with others for pure and simple fun. Americans need social dance communities in an era where jobs separate extended families, garages separate neighbors, home entertainment systems replace the cinema, and televisions stifle communication among family members. The community dance represents a safe place to escape from regular life and experience the benefits of socialization and physical touch. People from the dance communities described in this book can travel virtually anywhere in North America and find people who are like them. It is not uncommon for these dancers to carpool with strangers, share a room with a stranger for a weekend or convention, or accept an invitation to stay overnight at a stranger's home. Through affiliation with a dance community, people can experience a sense of belonging on a national, sometimes international, level. People who otherwise would be strangers often become immediate friends.

Glossary

active couple: The couple in a group dance to whom the caller directs the calls.

animal dances: A series of improvisatory social dances of African American origin set to Ragtime music in the early 20th century.

Balkan dance: An International Folk Dance term that encompasses dance forms primarily from Bulgaria, Croatia, Greece, Macedonia, Romania, and Serbia. Most of the dances are done in serpentine or circular group formations.

ballet: An art form that developed in European courts during the Renaissance and was refined in France under the reign of King Louis XIV in the 17th century.

Big Circle Dance: Southern Appalachian Square Dance for any number of dancers in a circle. The caller alternates figures for the entire group with figures for small sets of dancers.

blackface minstrelsy: A popular 19th-century comedy show in which performers darkened their skin with burnt cork and depicted African American caricatures.

Buck and Wing: An African American plantation dance that combined Buck Dance and Pigeon Wing. Also, a pre–Tap Dance style popular in blackface minstrelsy.

Buck Dance: An African American plantation dance. Also, a generic term for a solo step dance in southern Appalachia.

character dance: A dance that usually has ballet elements and depicts a particular persona through movement, attire, props, and music.

Clogging: A step dance from the British Isles. Also, a generic term for southern Appalachian step dance forms.

Contra Dance: New England Square Dance in circle, square, and longways sets. The term often refers to just longways dances.

Contradanse Française: A French court dance in square formation that evolved from English Country Dance. It was popular in 18th-century Europe.

Cotillon: A French court dance in square formation that evolved from a French peasant dance. In the 19th century, the term became associated with a ballroom game with hundreds of figures, partner changing, and prizes.

country dance: A dance for couples in any sort of group formation.

Country Line Dance: A 1990s Line Dance craze to country-western music.

Danse Anglaise: The French name for English Country Dance when it was brought to France in the late 17th century. The French associated Danse Anglaise with longways sets.

duple minor: Two-couple subsets in a longways dance, so that couples number 1,2,1,2,1,2, and so on, for the length of the set.

Écossaise: A group dance in 2/4 time to Scottish music that was popular in European ballrooms in the late 18th and early 19th centuries.

English Country Dance: A type of group dance in square, circle, and longways sets first docuemnted in 1651 by John Playford and done in European courts in the 17th and 18th centuries.

exhibition: Performance or demonstration for an audience.

fad dance: A short-lived dance often tied to a specific song.

Flat-footing: see Buck Dance.

Foxtrot: An early 20th-century couple dance to Ragtime music popularized by Vernon and Irene Castle.

Galop: A 19th-century ballroom dance in 2/4 time that consisted of a series of *chassés* across the room.

Galopade: A variation of the Galop.

heads: Two couples' positions in a square set, standing with backs toward the caller and facing the caller.

honors: Bows and curtseys.

Hula: Hawaiian dance ritual commercialized for tourism and entertainment in the 19th and early 20th century. It went through a traditional revival in the 1970s.

improper formation: A longways formation where some partners cross over, or change positions, within the set so that lines do not consist entirely of the same sex, as in a proper formation.

inactive couple: A couple in a group dance to whom the caller does not direct the calls. This couple observes and sometimes helps the active couple through the figures.

International Folk Dance: A recreational club-based folk dance movement that includes dances from many lands. Most RIFD groups in the 21st century focus on Balkan dance.

Israeli dance: A dance movement that became popular among people of Jewish heritage in the late 1940s. The dances were recognized as recent inventions, included elements of modern dance, and carried over into International Folk Dance repertoire.

Jig: Solo step dance form from the British Isles. Also a type of Buck Dance and Irish dance.

Lancers Quadrille: A type of Quadrille popular after the Plain Quadrille, characterized by five parts and the following meters: Part I, 6/8; Part II, 2/4; Part III, 6/8; Part IV, 6/8; and Part V, 4/4. It often concluded with a marching figure.

Line Dance: A nonpartner social dance movement in the 1950s and 1960s that experienced a resurgence in the 1990s with country-western music.

longways: A group formation that consists of two parallel lines. Some longways sets are for a specific number of couples. The most popular longways sets are for "as many as will," meaning any number of couples can join the set.

Mazurka: A 19th-century ballroom dance that originated in Poland, with leaps, stamps, and glides in 3/4 time.

mixer: A dance that involves partner changing.

Modern English Country Dance: New English Country Dance choreography in the Playford style. It is slower than Contra Dance, has a balletic quality, and often is done in triple meter.

Modern Western Square Dance: A recreational dance movement that developed in the 1960s, characterized by unpredictable choreography where all dancers move simultaneously.

Morris Dance: An old English dance form traditionally done by groups of men for ritual celebrations.

national dance: A dance that is well known within a nation.

old-time music: Acoustic string band music characteristic of rural America in the early 20th century.

One-Step: A dance that entails simple walking. A refined version of the Turkey Trot.

patter call: A type of Square Dance call that can be done to a variety of songs. The caller chants the dance instructionsand completes verbal phrases with noninstructional words (patter).

Pigeon Wing: see Buck Dance.

Plain Quadrille: The most popular type of Quadrille in the early 19th century. The most common form, popularized at Almack's in London, consisted of four Contradanse figures and one Cotillon figure: Le Pantelon, L'Été, La Poule, La Frenis, and Le Final.

Playford dances: The original English Country Dances, popularized by Cecil Sharp as part of the folk dance movement in the early 20th century.

play-party game: An adaptation of European dances in parts of the United States impacted by 19th-century evangelical religious revivals that forbade dancing and condemned the fiddle as the devil's instrument.

Polka: A 19th-century ballroom dance form believed to have originated in Bohemia, with the basic pattern of hop-step-close-step twice, alternating feet, in 2/4 time.

popular dance: A dance that is well known to the public.

Powwow: An intertribal dance event among Native Americans that became popular in the 1950s.

program: All the activities at a dance event, preplanned by a master of ceremonies or caller.

progression: The process of moving to a sequential position within the set, common in English Country Dance, Scottish Country Dance, and Contra Dance.

proper formation: A longways formation in which, when facing the caller, men are in the left line and women are in the right line, partners next to each other.

Quadrille: A ballroom dance in square formation popular throughout Europe and North America in the 19th century, revived by Henry Ford in the early 20th century.

Recreational Square Dance: A club-based activity that borrowed rural dance forms for urban recreation, starting in the 1940s.

Redowa: A Waltz-like dance that may have originated from the Mazurka. The foundation of the Redowa is the Polish Pas de Basque in 3/4 time, one of the four basic Mazurka steps.

Ring Shout: African American dance form in Baptist churches. It entails traveling in a circle, and participants must not cross feet.

ritual dance: Dance where the purpose is to communicate with a greater power in order to achieve a desirable outcome.

Round Dance: The couple dances popular in Modern Western Square Dance venues.

Schottische: A 19th-century ballroom dance that may have originated from the Bavarian Polka or Écossaise. The basic step pattern consists of close-step-hop twice, leading with alternating feet, followed by four step-hops in a circle.

set: Any type of group formation (e.g. circle, square, longways).

Shuffling: see Buck Dance.

sides: Two couples' positions in a square set, standing perpendicular to the caller.

singing call: A call for which the caller harmonizes the instructions to a specific song's melody and often sings the actual song lyrics during calls that take several counts to complete.

social dance: A dance where the primary purpose is to interact with people in a fun recreational setting, with or without formal instruction.

Square Dance: Group dance forms in rural parts of North America that mainly evolved from European dance figures. The caller, who prompts the dances in real time, is a unique American invention that distinguishes American Square Dance from similar European dance forms.

theatrical dance: A dance intended to be aesthetic for audience appeal.

traditional dance: A dance that endures over time, from generation to generation.

triple minor: Three-couple subsets in a longways dance, so that couples number 1,2,3,1,2,3, etc., for the length of the set.

Two-Step: A late 19th-century American ballroom dance form that flourished largely because of its simplicity and John Philip "March King" Sousa's military and patriotic marches.

Varsovienne: A 19th-century ballroom couple dance with characteristics of Polish dance that uses a basic pattern of sweep-glide-close.

Visiting Couple dance: A type of Square Dance characteristic of the West. An active couple goes around the square and does a figure with the inactive couples, one at a time. At certain points in the dance, everyone dances at the same time in a group figure.

Waltz: A revolutionary 19th-century ballroom dance in 3/4 time that uses a closed-position embrace that originally was highly controversial.

References

American Folklife Center. http://www.loc.gov/folklife/archive.html

American Life Histories. http://memory.loc.gov/ammem/wpaintro/wpahome.html

Anderson, Virginia C. *Square and Circle*. Woodbury, New Jersey: American Squares, 1950.

Bealle, John. *Old-Time Music and Dance: Community and Folk Revival*. Bloomington: Indiana University Press, 2005.

Born in Slavery. http://memory.loc.gov/ammem/snhtml/snhome.html

Burchenal, Elizabeth. *American Country-Dances: Twenty-Eight Contra-Dances Largely from the New England States*. New York: G. Schirmer, 1918.

Burchenal, Elizabeth. *Folk Dances from Old Homelands*. New York: Barnes, 1922.

CALLERLAB, Callerlab.org.

Casey, Betty. *International Folk Dancing U.S.A.* Garden City, NY: Doubleday, 1981.

Castle, Irene. *Castles in the Air: As Told to Bob and Wanda Duncan*. Garden City, NY: Doubleday, 1958.

Castle, Vernon and Irene. *Modern Dancing*. New York: Harper, 1914.

Cellarius, Henri. *Drawing Room Dances*. London: E. Churton, 1847.

Chujoy, Anatole. *The Dance Encyclopedia*. New York: Barnes, 1949.

C.L.O.G., http://www.clog.org/

Cohen, Selma Jeanne, ed. *International Encyclopedia of Dance*. New York: Oxford University Press, 2004.

Coll, Charles J. *Dancing Made Easy*. New York: Clode, 1919.

Dannett, Sylvia, and Frank Rachel. *Down Memory Lane: Arthur Murray's Picture Story of Social Dancing*. New York: Greenberg, 1954.

Dawson, Bob, and Don Bell. *The Keys to Calling Square Dances*. Florida: Don Bell and Bob Dawson, 1961.

Dodworth, Allen. *Dancing and Its Relation to Education and Social Life*. New York: Harper, 1885.

Duggan, Anne Schley. *Tap Dances*. New York: Barnes, 1936.

Duggan, Anne Schley, Jeanette Schlottmann, and Abbie Rutledge. *Folk Dances of the United States and Mexico*. New York: Barnes, 1948.

Duke, Jerry. *Clog Dance in the Appalachians*. San Francisco: Duke, 1984.

Duke, Jerry. *Dances of the Cajuns*. San Francisco: Duke, 1987.

Dunham, Katherine. *Dances of Haiti*. Los Angeles: Center for Afro-American Studies at UCLA, 1983.

Durlacher, Ed. *Honor Your Partner: Eighty-One American Square, Circle and Contra Dances, with Complete Instructions for Doing Them*. New York: The Devin-Adair Company, 1949.

Ehrenreich, Barbara. *Dancing in the Streets: A History of Collective Joy*. New York: Henry Holt, Metropolitan, 2006.

Emery, Lynne Fauley. *Black Dance from 1619 to Today*. Princeton, NJ: Dance Horizons, Princeton, 1988.

Folk-News 8, no. 1/2 (September–October 1939).

Ford, Henry. *Good Morning: After a Sleep of Twenty-Five Years, Old-Fashioned Dancing Is Being Revived by Mr. and Mrs. Ford*. Dearborn, MI: Dearborn, 1926.

Frost, Helen. *Tap, Caper, and Clog*. New York: Barnes, 1931.

Giordano, Ralph G. *Social Dancing in America: A History and Reference*. Westport, CT: Greenwood, 2007.

Graetz, Martin. "Pinewoods Morris Men." 1989. http://www.pinewoodsmorris.org/history.html

Greene, Hank. *Square and Folk Dancing: A Complete Guide for Students, Teachers, and Callers*. New York: Harper & Row, 1984.

Grove, Lilly. *Dancing*. London: Longmans, Green, 1907.

Gulick, Luther H. *The Healthful Art of Dancing*. New York: Doubleday, Page, 1910.

Haenni, Sabine. *The Immigrant Scene: Ethnic Amusements in New York 1880–1920*. Minneapolis: University of Minnesota Press, 2008.

Hall, J. Tillman. *Dance! A Complete Guide to Social, Folk & Square Dancing*. Belmont, CA: Wadsworth, 1963.

Hamilton, Frank. *Roundance Manual for Callers, Teachers, Club Committees, and Dancers*. Los Angeles: Sets in Order, 1962.

Harris, Jane A., Anne Pittman, and Marlys S. Waller. *Dance a While: A Handbook of Folk, Square, and Social Dance*. 7th ed. Boston: Allyn and Bacon, 1994.

Herman, Michael. *Folk Dancer* 1, no. 5 (July 1941).

Herman, Michael. *Folk Dancer* 2, no. 6 (June 1943).

Herman, Michael. *Folk Dancer* 3, no. 6 (June 1944).

Hinman, Mary Wood. *Gymnastics and Folk Dancing, Volume 5*. New York: Barnes: 1918.

Holden, Rickey. *The Contra Dance Book*. Newark, NJ: American Squares, 1956.

Houston. *Folk Dance Problem Solver*. Austin, TX: Society of Folk Dance Historians, 2004.

Houston. *Folk Dance Problem Solver*. Austin, TX: Society of Folk Dance Historians, 2006.

Indian Pueblo Cultural Center. www.indianpueblo.org

Jackson, Naomi M. *Converging Movements: Modern Dance and Jewish Culture at the 92nd Street Y*. Hanover, NH: University Press of New England, 2000.

Knowles, Mark. *Tap Roots: The Early History of Tap Dancing*. Jefferson, NC, and London: McFarland, 2002.

Laušević, Mirjana. *Balkan Fascination: Creating an Alternative Music Culture in America*. New York: Oxford University Press, 2007.

Leonard, Fiona. "The Legend of the Smoki Indian." March 12, 2009. http://www.yearinamerica.net/2009/03/legend-of-smoki-indian.html

Longley, Grant F. *Line Dance Manual*. Norwell, MA: New England Caller, 1977.

Marron, Graeme, and Anna Marron. *Square Dancing for Young and Old*. New York: Padell, 1944.

Mayo, Jim. *Step by Step Through Modern Square Dance History*. Bloomington, IN: Jim Mayo, 2003.

Mayo, Margot. *The American Square Dance: Calls and Music with Illustrated Description of Figures for Folk and Country Dances*. New York: Sentinel, 1943.

Millstone, David. *The Other Way Back: Dancing with Dudley*. DVD. Lebanon, NH: Farnum Hill, 2007.

National Council for the Traditional Arts. http://www.ncta.net

Needham, Maureen, ed. *I See America Dancing: Select Readings 1685–2000*. Chicago: University of Illinois Press, 2002.

Nevell, Richard. *A Time to Dance: American Country Dancing from Hornpipe to Hot Hash*. New York: St. Martin's, 1977.

New England Folk Festival Association. http://www.neffa.org/

New School for Social Research. http://www.newschool.edu/nssr/

Owens, Lee. *American Square Dances of the West and Southwest*. Palo Alto, CA: Pacific, 1949.

Page, Ralph. *Heritage Dances of Early America*. Colorado Springs, CO: Century One, 1976.

Parkes, Tony. "In Praise of Herbie Gaudreau." 1996. http://www.io.com/~entropy/contradance/articles/in-praise-of-herbie.html

Playford, John. *The English Dancing-Master; or, Plaine and Easie Rules for the Dancing of Country Dances, with the Tune to Each Dance*. London: John Playford, 1651.

Ricciotti, Chris. "Welcome to Gender-Free Dancing." 2006. http://lcfd.org/Articles/GFManual/GF-Manual.pdf

Richardson, Philip J. S. *The Social Dances of the Nineteenth Century in England*. London: Herbert Jenkins, 1960.

Rossoff, Martin. *Hoedown Heritage: The Evolution of Modern Square Dancing*. Sandusky, OH: Burdick Enterprises, American Square Dance Magazine, 1977.

Round Dancing. http://www.rounddancing.net/dance/index.html

Shafter, Mary Severance. *American Indian and Other Folk Dances*. New York: Barnes, 1927.

Shaw, Lloyd. *Cowboy Dances: A Collection of Western Square Dances*. Caldwell, ID: Caxton, 1948.

Shaw, Lloyd. *The Round Dance Book*. Caldwell, ID: Caxton, 1949.

Shay, Anthony. *Choreographic Politics: State Folk Dance Companies, Representation, and Power*. Middletown, CT: Wesleyan University Press, 2002.

Shay, Anthony. *Dancing Across Borders: The American Fascination with Exotic Dance Forms*. Jefferson, NC, and London: McFarland, 2008.

Sickels, Alice L. *Around the World in St. Paul*. Minneapolis: University of Minnesota Press, 1945.

Smith, Mark K. "Ernest Thompson Seton and Woodcraft." 2002. http://www.infed.org/thinkers/seton.htm

Smukler, David, and David Millstone. *Cracking Chestnuts: The Living Tradition of Classic American Contra Dances*. Haydenville, MA: Country Dance and Song Society, 2008.

Stanley, S. C., and D. M. Lowery. *Manual of Gymnastic Dancing*. New York: Association Press and International Committee of Young Men's Christian Associations, 1920.

Steiner, Jesse F. *Studies in the Social Aspects of the Depression*. Stony Brook, NY: Arno, 1972.

Tolman, Beth, and Ralph Page. *The Country Dance Book*. New York: Barnes, 1937.

Tomko, Linda J. *Dancing Class: Gender, Ethnicity, and Social Divides in American Dance, 1890–1920*. Bloomington: Indiana University Press, 1999.

Vandervoort, Thea A. "The Dances of Early California in Santa Barbara." *UCI Undergraduate Research Journal*. 1999. Irvine: California: University of California at Irvine Center for Learning through the Arts and Technology. http://www.escholarship.org/uc/item/0v71t3xn.

Vissicaro, Pegge. *Studying Dance Cultures Around the World: An Introduction to Multicultural Dance Education*. Dubuque, IA: Kendall/Hunt, 2004.

Walkowitz, Daniel J. *City Folk: English Country Dance and the Politics of the Folk in Modern America*. New York University Press, 2010.

World Around Songs. http://www.worldaroundsongs.com.

Index

About the Author

ERICA M. NIELSEN became passionate about dance as a child, taking lessons at Miss Julie Divan's Innovations Dance Studio in Burlington, Wisconsin. She attended Macalester College in St. Paul, Minnesota, and majored in international studies with a focus in cultural anthropology, but most of her time was spent in the dance studio. In 2003, Nielsen combined her interests in anthropology and dance for a master's of fine arts degree in dance from Arizona State University. Her graduate work took her to Bulgaria and culminated in the publication of an essay, "Bulgarian Dance Culture: From Censorship to Chalga," in Anthony Shay's *Balkan Dance* (2008). After living in Boston for two years and performing with the Bulgarian folk dance ensemble Ludo Mlado, Nielsen returned to Phoenix, Arizona. She lives with her wonderful husband, Nicholas Okamura, who also enjoys music and dance.